# WHY TO WORRY WHEN

## FOR EVERY DREAMER WHO'S READY TO RISE ABOVE WORRIES

SHRUTI MORE

Made with ♥ on the Notion Press Platform
www.notionpress.com

To every soul who has ever doubted their worth, questioned their path, or feared the unknown—this book is for you. May you find the courage to embrace life's possibilities and trust in your journey.

*"The worries of yesterday have faded away,
and the worries of tomorrow have not yet arrived.
Let go of the worries and live in the present."*

# Contents

# Contents

# Foreword

Life, as we know it, is unpredictable. We're often faced with crossroads, uncertainties, and moments that challenge the very core of who we are. Yet, within these challenges lies an opportunity—an invitation to grow, to learn, and to realize that worry doesn't define our destiny. This book isn't a guide; it's a companion for those moments when doubt creeps in, making you wonder if you're enough.

I wrote this book not because I have all the answers but because I've asked the same questions you have. This book is for those navigating the pivotal years between 18 and 25, a time when you're expected to figure out who you are and where you're headed. It's for every young adult who has ever felt overwhelmed by the weight of choices, the sting of rejection, or the fear of failure. I've written this for the version of me who once stood in your shoes, grappling with the same uncertainties and striving to make sense of it all.

Each chapter is a reflection of lessons learned, insights gained, and the gentle yet powerful reminder that you have everything you need to navigate life's complexities. This is not just a book to be read; it's a conversation, a call to action, and a source of reassurance. It's here to remind you that worry may knock at the door, but courage, self-belief, and perspective are the keys to keeping it at bay.

As you turn these pages, my hope is that you'll find yourself nodding in recognition, smiling at the relatable anecdotes, and feeling a spark of inspiration to step forward, even when the path seems uncertain. This is your story, and this book is here to empower you to own it fully.

The journey is yours to take, and it begins right here, right now.

# Author's Note

Each chapter in this book is unique, crafted to address different aspects of life's journey. While the chapters can stand alone, I encourage you to read them in sequence. This order mirrors the progression of worries and challenges that often arise as we grow, helping you connect with the themes and experiences presented.

As you turn each page, I hope you find moments that resonate deeply, sparking self-reflection and inspiration. This book is more than just a collection of thoughts; it's a companion—here to offer you a reality check, provide motivation, and remind you that your journey is your own to shape and cherish.

# Acknowledgements

I am deeply grateful to everyone who supported me, cheered me on, and believed in me. To my family, for their unwavering encouragement and love; to my mentors, for their guidance and wisdom; and to my friends, for their constant support and faith. To every person who inspired me, challenged me, or stood by my side—thank you for being a part of my story. This book is a reflection of all the support and belief I've been fortunate to receive, and I am endlessly thankful for it.

CHAPTER I

# Why to Worry When Decision Determines Destiny

Every choice we make, no matter how small, sets the course for our future. It's a simple truth that can feel both empowering and overwhelming. From the mundane decision of what to eat for breakfast to the life-altering choices of career paths, relationships, or moving to a new city, each decision shapes the mosaic of our lives. But here's the thing: while the weight of making the "right" decision can feel paralyzing, the beauty lies in the fact that every choice is a stepping stone to growth, learning, and self-discovery.

Think about it—life is not a straight path. It's a winding road filled with twists, turns, and crossroads. At every junction, we're faced with decisions. Some may seem insignificant, like choosing between tea or coffee, while others feel monumental, like selecting a college major or accepting a job offer. What's common is this: every decision adds to the narrative of who we are and where we're headed.

At some point in our lives, we are all faced with moments of choice, where the decisions we make have the power to shape our future. These decisions, whether small or life-altering, have a cumulative effect on where we end up. The notion that "Decision Determines Destiny" is not just a philosophical concept but a reality that has proven true time and again for individuals across different walks of life.

One of the most critical moments where this concept comes into play is during our formative years. The path we choose in education, the career we aspire to pursue, and even the people we surround ourselves with can dramatically impact the trajectory of our lives. While some decisions seem minor at the time, they can compound into life-defining moments.

Take, for instance, the transition from school to the next level of education. This is a period filled with choices—whether to continue studying, which stream or subject to pursue, and what career to aim for. For many, this decision comes with immense pressure. The pressure to make the right choice and the fear of failure can cloud our judgment. In such moments, it's essential to remind ourselves that our decisions shape our destiny.

The Overwhelming Pressure of Choice.For most of us, there's a point in life where we're confronted with what seems like an insurmountable decision: what path should we take after school? Should we pursue science, commerce, or the arts? Which career offers the best opportunities? These are daunting questions, especially when society and familial expectations come into play.

Often, we seek the counsel of parents, relatives, and friends. In trying to get as much advice as possible, it's easy to become overwhelmed by the varied opinions we receive. Everyone has an idea of what they believe is best, but in the end, the decision rests solely on us. It's in these moments that we realize no one else can decide our future for us. Others can offer guidance, but it's our decision that defines our destiny.

One misconception that holds many of us back is the belief that only those who were naturally gifted or who have excelled throughout their academic life are destined for success. We may think that success is reserved for those who were "born" to excel. This mindset often becomes a roadblock, creating unnecessary self-doubt and anxiety. The truth is, success isn't determined by inherent abilities alone but by consistent effort and determination.

Realizing the Power of Hard Work. For many, the realization that hard work can bridge the gap between potential and achievement marks a turning point in life. There may have been moments when it seemed like no matter how much effort was put into studying, success was elusive. This can lead to the false belief that certain achievements, such as scoring high marks or getting into a prestigious field, are beyond reach unless you are naturally gifted.

But what many fail to realize is that the combination of hard work and perseverance is the key to unlocking one's true potential. As one starts to see incremental progress—whether in better grades or improved skills—the myth of "born genius" begins to unravel. The process of growth itself becomes a motivator, and the idea that success is attainable for anyone who is willing to put in the work starts to take root.

It's here that the decision to persevere and continue pushing forward begins to shape destiny. Once the mind shifts from worrying about what others have accomplished to focusing on what is possible through one's own efforts, the journey truly begins. This is where decision meets destiny, and the results start to manifest.

One of the biggest roadblocks to success is self-doubt. It's easy to fall into the trap of comparing yourself to others—especially those who seem to achieve success effortlessly. In the modern world, where social media often showcases only the highlights of people's lives, it's easy to feel inadequate or incapable. However, comparing yourself to others is rarely a constructive exercise.

The crucial decision here is to cultivate self-belief. No one is born with endless self-confidence. It's something that is developed over time, often through trial and error. By choosing to believe in yourself and your abilities, you are already taking a significant step toward shaping your future. There is a famous quote, often attributed to Henry Ford, that says, "Whether you think you can or you think you can't—you're right."

When you decide to believe in yourself, you stop worrying about the limitations others might see in you, and you start focusing on what you are capable of achieving. This shift in mindset can be transformational. Belief is a powerful tool that can fuel your determination and keep you focused on your goals, no matter how difficult they may seem.

A common myth is that only certain paths lead to success—namely, careers in Medicine, Engineering, or similar prestigious fields. While these careers are certainly respected, they are not the only paths to success. The world is full of diverse opportunities, and success can be achieved in any field as long as there is passion and determination behind it. The most important thing is to choose a path that excites and inspires you, rather than one that you feel compelled to take due to external pressures.

We often hear about the struggles of certain professions, such as the oversaturation of engineers in some countries. This reality may deter some from pursuing what they truly love. But the key is not to shy away from a field due to fear of competition, but to embrace it with the understanding that success comes from perseverance and innovation. No field is immune to challenges, but with the right mindset, you can carve out a unique space for yourself in any industry.

Another powerful tool in shaping your destiny is visualization. The concept of the Law of Attraction has gained popularity in recent years, but its roots are ancient. The idea is simple: when you clearly define what you want and focus your energy on it, the universe conspires to help you achieve it.

There are countless stories of individuals who wrote down their goals or created vision boards and, with time and effort, saw those dreams become a reality. The simple act of writing down your aspirations can bring clarity and direction. It's a decision that signals to both your subconscious and the world around you that you are committed to your goals.

This practice of visualization can be immensely motivating. By clearly defining what success looks like for you—whether it's a specific career, personal achievement, or life milestone—you give yourself a target to aim for. It's no longer about vague hopes and dreams; it becomes a tangible goal that you are working toward every day.

The important take away here is that the decision to set goals and visualize success is a step toward making those goals a reality. While visualization alone is not enough—hard work and persistence are crucial—the act of clearly defining your ambitions can be a powerful catalyst for success.

No journey toward success is without its challenges. Life has a way of throwing unexpected obstacles in our path, and it's easy to feel discouraged when things don't go according to plan. In these moments, the decisions we make can either set us back or propel us forward.

Choosing to see obstacles as opportunities for growth is a critical decision that shapes our destiny. When faced with a challenge, you have two options: you can allow it to defeat you, or you can rise to the occasion and learn from it. Those who achieve great success in life are not those who never encounter failure, but those who learn from it and use it to fuel their determination.

There will always be moments of self-doubt and fear, but it's important to remember that every challenge is an opportunity in disguise. It's through overcoming obstacles that we grow stronger, more resilient, and more prepared for the future.

The Impact of Support Systems. Another key factor in determining your destiny is the people you surround yourself with. No one achieves success entirely on their own. Behind every successful individual is a support system of friends, family, mentors, and peers who provide encouragement, guidance, and belief in their potential.

Deciding to lean on your support system is not a sign of weakness; it's a smart decision that many overlook. When you surround yourself with people who believe in your potential, who push you to be better, and who lift you up when you feel down, you are setting yourself up for success.

At the same time, it's important to be mindful of the people you allow into your inner circle. Negative influences, those who doubt your abilities or discourage your dreams, can hold you back. It's crucial to make the decision to distance yourself from negativity and instead focus on those who will help you grow.

Decision-making is a skill that shapes your life, influencing both major milestones and everyday progress. It's not a one-time event but a continuous process that develops over time. To enhance your decision-making, start by evaluating the consequences of each choice—considering the pros and cons—and learning from the outcomes. Begin with small decisions, as making too many choices each day can lead to a decline in decision quality, a phenomenon known as decision fatigue. By focusing on fewer but more meaningful decisions, you'll improve your ability to handle larger, more impactful choices with confidence and clarity.

In the end, the most important decision you can make is to take ownership of your life. It's easy to fall into the trap of thinking that life happens to us, that our circumstances define our future. But the truth is, it's our decisions that shape our destiny.

Whether it's choosing a career path, setting goals, overcoming obstacles, or believing in yourself, every decision you make moves you closer to the future you want. Success is not something that happens by accident; it's the result of deliberate choices, consistent effort, and unwavering belief in your potential.

So, why worry when you have the power to shape your destiny through your decisions?

The path to success is not always clear, and it's rarely easy. But with the right mindset, determination, and belief in your abilities, there is no limit to what you can achieve.

The decisions you make today will determine where you end up tomorrow. Choose wisely, and trust that your destiny is in your hands.

In the grand scheme of life, no decision is as monumental as we often make it out to be. Yes, choosing a stream or a career path is important, but it's not the only factor that will determine your future success. What matters most is your willingness to work hard, to adapt when necessary, and to never stop believing in your potential.

The journey to success is not determined by a single choice, but by a series of decisions that build upon one another. As long as you remain open to learning and growing, you will continue to move forward.

Ultimately, it's not the decisions we make that shape our destiny, but the way we approach them. When we recognize our potential, work hard, and remain resilient in the face of challenges, we are actively creating the future we desire. Decision determines destiny, but it's the belief in yourself that will carry you to the heights you were always meant to reach.

CHAPTER II

# Why to Worry When Change Is a Catalyst for Growth

Change is often a double-edged sword. It's something many people crave when they feel stuck, bored, or uninspired, hoping for something new to break up the monotony of daily routines. Yet, when change arrives in a form that disrupts comfort zones—pushing us into unfamiliar territory—what once seemed refreshing can quickly feel overwhelming and uncomfortable. However, it is precisely this discomfort that often holds the potential for our greatest growth.

Consider life changes like moving away from home for education or a job. Suddenly, the everyday comforts we took for granted—home-cooked meals, familiar faces, and routines—are replaced with cafeteria food, roommates, and entirely new environments. The transition from being in a space where people understand and know us intimately to one where we're just getting to know others can feel isolating and challenging. Adjusting to this new normal is difficult, but it's also an opportunity to develop resilience, adaptability, and self-reliance.

Beyond environmental changes, personal growth often requires shifts in goals and aspirations. As we progress through life, our ambitions evolve, and so do our paths to achieve them. Goals we once considered unchangeable may shift with time, and sometimes, big decisions become essential to moving forward. Change in priorities and perspectives nudges us to make those tough choices—whether it's pursuing a different career, moving to a new city, or making sacrifices for a new dream. Each decision made in the face of change helps shape our future, revealing new strengths and capacities within us.

Instead of resisting change, viewing it as a learning journey can transform our experience. By embracing the new and unknown, we allow ourselves to grow in ways we couldn't anticipate, leading to personal insights, stronger self-awareness, and an expanded vision of what we can achieve.

From the time I was little, my life has been a whirlwind of change. Growing up surrounded by family, I was cheerful and happy, always surrounded by familiar faces. But things took a sudden turn when, at just eight years old, I was sent to live with my maternal grandparents for school. Although I was surrounded by their love, I missed my parents and my younger brother terribly. My brother always wanted me around, and it broke my heart to be apart from him. I would often cry quietly, feeling that deep, lonely ache whenever I thought of home. Yet, even at that age, I somehow knew I had to adapt. I put on a brave face for my family, never letting my parents see how much I missed them.

Living in my grandparents' countryside village added its own set of challenges. My school was 23 kilometers away, and the day started early. My grandmother would wake up at 5:00 a.m. to prepare breakfast and lunch for me, heating water for my bath in an old-fashioned copper vessel. This utensil was unique—big, heavy, and built for the countryside life. She'd fill it with wood, light a fire underneath, and carefully tend to it until the water was warm enough for me to bathe before my long day at school.

As I grew, so did my experiences with change. After graduating from my school in the village, my family decided I would move to my uncle's town for 11th and 12th grades. Since my uncle was a principal at a military school, he helped me get into a college with good connections. For the first time, I asked to stay in a hostel. I felt ready for a little independence and was tired of feeling like I was always in someone else's home.

Moving to a hostel was another test. I was used to the warmth and safety of family, so it was an emotional shift. I had to adapt to a new social environment, new people, and a shared living space. During my hostel days, life was a mix of fun, mischief, and lessons learned. My roommates were generally nice, but I was so gentle and accommodating that I often felt hurt if someone spoke to me rudely. Over time, though, I toughened up—a lot! Eventually, I found myself standing up for everything, even the smallest things, like hot water for my morning bath. It might sound trivial now, but at that time, it felt empowering.

One thing that really stirred up the hostel was my love for cats. I'd feed them and even sneak them into my room from time to time. My roommates weren't exactly thrilled with this feline arrangement, to put it lightly! I'd hear all sorts of protests, but that didn't stop me. In fact, I was called into the rector's office multiple times, receiving stern lectures about "responsibility" and "rules."

Then there was the time they even called my uncle to talk some sense into me. It was meant to be a "serious" intervention, but honestly, I found it pretty amusing. I'd sit there listening, nodding respectfully, while inside, I knew I wasn't going to change a thing. Sure, I'd feel emotional at the moment, but a few tears didn't stop me from going back to my stubborn ways afterward.

In hostel life, I developed my own rule: if someone treated me well, I'd do the same for them. Maybe that's why people were mostly nice to me, at least on the surface. Some friendships were truly genuine, though, and I cherished those. Since I'd scored well in my 10$^{th}$ grade exams, I felt this underlying pressure to maintain those grades, even when I didn't really want to.

Weekends were always eventful, too. While other students had their parents visiting them, I'd sometimes get a visit from my uncle—not for a casual chat, but because he'd been called in for my "misdeeds." Looking back, I can laugh about it now, but back then, those moments felt intense, adding to the unique, rebellious chapter that was my hostel life.

The biggest transition, however, was in academics. I had worked hard for my 10$^{th}$-grade exams, driven to prove myself and justify my decision to live away from my family. This academic success brought expectations—to maintain that standard. Despite not being a top student, I knew that the real goal was personal growth, not perfection. Even in the hostel, where it was common for students' parents to visit every weekend with treats, I never expected my family to visit, but they did. My dad always brought me my favorite treat, gulab jamun, and they'd leave with smiles, hiding any sadness they felt. Years later, my mom told me that on the first day they left me at the hostel, my dad pulled over just a few miles away, unable to hold back his tears.

With COVID-19, another wave of change swept over my life. Classes moved online, and I struggled with the isolation, disorganized lessons, and the lack of accountability in tests and assignments. I felt the urgency of finding a backup plan when my NEET score wasn't sufficient for an MBBS course, which was my original goal simply because I didn't like math. I turned to engineering as an alternative and began brushing up on the basics for the MHT-CET entrance exam. When the results came out, I was relieved to see that I'd scored well enough for admission to a good engineering college. That moment felt like a reminder that sometimes, the universe has other plans that are better suited to us.

Now in my third year of engineering with a promising internship offer, I look back on the journey of constant change and adaptation with a deep sense of gratitude. Each stage, each new place, and each unfamiliar environment taught me resilience and self-reliance. I realized that change, though it often feels like a storm, has a way of clearing paths and uncovering new aspects of ourselves.

If you can relate to this story, you're not alone. We all face changes that shape us, whether they're exciting, intimidating, or bittersweet. Embracing change instead of resisting it allows us to transform and grow. Each change prepares us for a future that might otherwise seem overwhelming. So, the next time change knocks on your door, welcome it with open arms. Trust that it's not here to make your life harder, but to make you stronger, more adaptable, and ready for the limitless possibilities that lie ahead.

Life is full of transformations — a journey marked by changes in behavior, appearance, style, communication, and our perspective of the world. These changes are natural and inevitable, yet, what sets one apart is the ability to adapt thoughtfully to them, making each change a stepping stone to growth.

As we navigate these changes, our first task is understanding whether they are positive or negative influences on our lives. Once we have that clarity, we can confidently move forward, secure in our choices. This ability to discern enables us to align with positive changes and distance ourselves from the ones that could hinder our progress.

Mastering this skill makes us resilient; we learn to flow with life rather than resist its currents. The external environment, people, places, or situations may keep evolving, but they can no longer deter us. With an open mind, we can approach change not as a challenge but as a catalyst to strengthen us, to learn, and to thrive.Embracing change doesn't only propel us forward; it builds the strength to handle any transition, making each shift in our lives smoother and ultimately leading us closer to our goals.

"Never change yourself for others" — it's a saying that resonates with many. We've all heard it countless times, and it seems straightforward enough: stay true to who you are, no matter what others think or expect. This advice might feel empowering, like a personal shield against criticism and judgment, but it's worth taking a closer look. Why not change, if it's for the better?

Imagine a situation where someone suggests a change in your behavior or habits. Perhaps it's about learning to manage time more efficiently, becoming more patient, or even taking better care of yourself. Now, if this change could bring positivity to your life or help you grow, then is it still unwise to consider it, simply because it originated from someone else? Often, we get stuck in our own perspective, thinking that changing for others would somehow mean losing a part of ourselves or compromising our "authenticity." But here's the twist: sometimes, the encouragement from others can be the push we need toward self-improvement, and ignoring these influences solely based on ego can mean missing out on something truly valuable.

Instead of blindly following this mantra of "never change for others," it might be more practical to examine each instance carefully. Ask yourself: Is this change beneficial? Could it help me grow or achieve something important? If so, why let pride stop you? Sometimes, our biggest obstacle is our own ego — the voice that insists we shouldn't have to change for anyone else. It convinces us that if we change because of someone else's suggestion, it somehow diminishes us. But in reality, a willingness to learn and adapt isn't a weakness; it's a strength.

Consider the story of a young professional who always took pride in being a "lone wolf." Working solo was comfortable and meant they never had to worry about relying on others. But over time, they started receiving feedback about how collaborative skills could enhance their career. At first, they dismissed it — after all, why change something so core to who they were? But gradually, they realized that shifting their approach could bring about growth in ways they hadn't considered. Embracing teamwork didn't make them any less of who they were; it only broadened their skills and deepened their impact.

So, perhaps the better approach is to stay open to change when it aligns with our goals and values, regardless of where the suggestion originates. Adjusting for others doesn't mean erasing our identity; instead, it's like adding another layer to who we are. We can remain authentic while still evolving. And here's where the freedom lies: choosing which changes to embrace and which to let pass by. It's not about bending to every request or criticism, but rather about being thoughtful and receptive to positive shifts, wherever they come from.

In a world where each experience, person, and perspective has something to teach us, let's rethink the mantra. Why not allow ourselves to change for the better, even if it's inspired by others? Instead of seeing it as compromise, let's view it as growth. Because, at the end of the day, if a change brings us closer to who we want to be, then that change is ours, not anyone else's. And in this openness to improvement lies a liberating truth: there's always room to grow, and sometimes, the best inspiration comes from others.

Change is the catalyst for growth. Every shift, every adaptation, and even every uncomfortable adjustment prepares us for the opportunities that lie ahead. Embracing change is like preparing the soil before planting seeds; it nurtures growth in ways we might not even realize in the moment.

Life has a way of presenting us with endless challenges, unexpected twists, and fresh chances to evolve. Each change is a stepping stone, shaping us to be stronger, wiser, and better equipped for the future. So, never resist the changes that life brings. Embrace them with an open heart and an open mind. Remember, it's through change that we grow far beyond what we think we're capable of. Change isn't just a part of life; it's what makes life a journey of endless discovery and self-transformation.

CHAPTER III

# Why to Worry When Your Journey Is Unique

In a world obsessed with benchmarks, comparisons, and "one-size-fits-all" success stories, it's easy to fall into the trap of worrying about where you stand. Are you ahead or behind? Are you doing things the "right" way? But here's a revolutionary idea: your journey is unique, and that's a reason to embrace it—not to worry.

One of the biggest myths we face is the belief in a "perfect timeline." Some people find their dream job right after graduation, while others take four or five years to do so. Some discover their true calling at 10, while others might not realize it until their 40s. Some marry at 25 and face divorce by 30, while others find lifelong love later on. This just goes to show that everyone's journey is unique, and that's the beauty of it. You are exactly where you're meant to be, so stop measuring yourself with someone else's ruler. Stop comparing yourself with others, because what you are going through may be something they haven't experienced. Likewise, the challenges they've faced might not be something you've encountered yet.

Your journey is unique because you face different obstacles, challenges, and circumstances. The way you deal with these challenges is different from others, and that's what shapes your path. Whether it's your career or your personal life, what's important is to "master yourself." Once you truly know yourself—your strengths, weaknesses, and desires—you can progress on your journey without the need to compare yourself to anyone else. The path that others follow may be paved with flowers for them, but it could be filled with thorns for you. So, stop following someone else's path and carve your own.

Imagine seashells scattered along the shore, each with its own shape, color, and texture. Some are smooth, others are ridged. Some shine brightly in the sun, while others carry muted tones. Yet, each shell is beautiful in its own way, shaped by the unique journey it has taken through the waves and tides. Your journey is like that seashell—shaped by your experiences, your struggles, and your triumphs. Comparing yourself to someone else is like trying to decide which seashell is better—it's pointless because their beauty lies in their individuality.

One of the most pervasive myths is that life follows a linear path—a predictable sequence of milestones and achievements. School, job, marriage, family, retirement. This framework works for some, but for many, life is more of a winding road filled with detours, pauses, and surprises.

When you compare your unique journey to a rigid, linear template, you're setting yourself up for unnecessary worry. Why? Because the template isn't designed for you. It doesn't account for your experiences, challenges, or dreams. It assumes that everyone's destination is the same, which couldn't be further from the truth.

Seeking advice or suggestions from others is fine, but in the end, you are the one who must plan your journey. People can lift you up or push you down, so take their advice with an open mind, but implement it in your own way. Remember, their advice is based on their experience, which may be helpful, but your journey is not the same as theirs. Stop comparing and never lose your individuality.

Each of us is born into different circumstances, with different challenges, talents, and opportunities. While it's natural to look around and compare yourself to others, doing so can often lead to a feeling of inadequacy or frustration. We may look at someone else's success and wonder why we haven't reached the same milestones, why our path seems more difficult or uncertain. But the truth is, everyone's journey is uniquely theirs, and trying to follow someone else's blueprint for life will only lead to dissatisfaction.

Everyone knows the day they were born, but once you discover why you were born and the reason for your existence, that's when you truly win in life. Knowing yourself and having the confidence to shape your journey as per your needs—while facing challenges in your own unique way—is what makes you special. So, why worry when your journey is unique? Let others succeed early, and be happy for them. They've grown at their own pace and now deserve their success. Use their achievements as motivation, and keep working to shape your own unique path.

The Power of Individual Timing. Have you ever felt like you're running out of time? Society often imposes invisible deadlines: graduate by this age, have a stable career by that age, and so on. But life doesn't come with a universal timetable. Some people discover their passions at 16, others at 60. Both are valid.

Take J.K. Rowling, who wrote her first Harry Potter book as a struggling single mother in her early 30s. Or Colonel Sanders, who founded KFC in his 60s. Their timelines didn't align with conventional expectations, but their journeys were no less remarkable. When you accept that your timing is your own, you free yourself from the pressure of external schedules.

Think about it: if you spend your time living according to someone else's expectations, you're not truly living your life. You're simply going through the motions of what you think is expected of you. This not only limits your potential but also stifles your happiness and fulfillment. Your journey is meant to be shaped by your experiences, your dreams, and your decisions—not someone else's.

Time is the most valuable resource we have, and once it's gone, we can never get it back. That's why it's so important to make the most of it by focusing on what truly matters to you.

Whether it's your career, your personal life, or your aspirations, only you can define what success looks like for you. And success doesn't necessarily mean achieving the same things as someone else. It could mean following a passion that others don't understand or taking a path that seems unconventional. What's important is that it's your path, shaped by your vision.

There's a beautiful freedom that comes with embracing the uniqueness of your journey. It frees you from the constant pressure of comparison and competition. When you stop measuring your worth against someone else's achievements, you allow yourself to focus on what truly makes you happy and fulfilled. What might seem like an easy road for someone else could be filled with unseen struggles, just as your journey may have challenges that others don't fully understand.

Loving your own journey means appreciating every step, regardless of what it gives you in return. Its about finding value in the lessons learned, the resilience built, and the growth achieved along the way. When you accept your path for a unique, unfolding story you free yourself from the need for external validation or immediate rewards. Instead, you cultivate a deeper connection to your experiences, recognizing that even the challenges enrich the narrative of your life. Loving your journey is not just about reaching a destination; its about cherishing the adventure itself.

By acknowledging the uniqueness of your journey, you give yourself permission to grow at your own pace. Some people achieve their dreams early in life, while others may take longer. Some face massive obstacles and setbacks, while others may have a smoother ride. But no matter what your path looks like, it's important to trust the process. Trust that every challenge you face is shaping you into the person you're meant to become. Trust that even when things don't go according to plan, they are still moving you closer to your ultimate goal. Every experience, every setback, and every victory contributes to your growth and success in ways you might not even realize at the moment.

At the end of the day, your journey is yours alone. You are the one who will experience its highs and lows, its joys and sorrows. No one else can walk it for you, and no one else can determine its outcome. By embracing this truth, you empower yourself to live more authentically and meaningfully. You stop worrying about whether you're keeping up with others or living up to their expectations, and instead focus on becoming the best version of yourself.

In the grand tapestry of life, no two journeys are the same—and that's what makes it extraordinary. Your path is yours alone, filled with moments, choices, and experiences that are uniquely designed for you. Comparing your journey to someone else's is like comparing stars in the sky; each shines in its own time and way. Embrace the detours, celebrate the milestones, and find beauty in the unexpected twists. Your story is unfolding exactly as it's meant to, and there's no need to worry when the journey is uniquely, wonderfully yours.

CHAPTER IV

# Why to Worry When Growth Comes from Challenges

Once upon a time, a young girl and her grandfather went to a plant nursery to buy some plants for their home. They spent hours visiting different nurseries, searching for plants that the girl liked. After a long search, they finally found two plants that were perfect for her. The girl was excited as she held the two small plants in her hands, imagining how they would grow and beautify their home.

As they returned home, the grandfather proposed a small experiment. He suggested planting one of the plants inside the house, where it would be protected and cared for, and the other in the backyard, where it would be exposed to the elements—sunlight, wind, and rain. Curious about what would happen, the girl agreed. After planting the two plants, her grandfather asked, "Which plant do you think will grow stronger?"

The girl confidently answered, "The one inside the house, of course. It will be safe from storms, harsh sunlight, and wind. The plant outside will struggle to survive."

Her grandfather smiled but said nothing, simply observing her reasoning.

Years passed, and one day, the girl returned to her grandfather's house. She had grown older and was now facing the challenges of deciding her future, just like many others. As they sat together in the backyard, her grandfather gently reminded her of their little experiment. He took her to see the two plants they had planted five years earlier.

To her surprise, the plant that had been inside the house had grown well, but it was still small and fragile. However, the plant that had been left outside had grown into a mighty tree. Its branches spread far and wide, and its thick trunk provided shade for anyone who walked by. Astonished, the girl asked, "How did this happen, Grandpa? I thought the plant inside the house would grow better because it was safe."

Her grandfather smiled warmly and replied, "Yes, the plant inside was safe, but it had limited space to grow. It never faced any real challenges or dangers. On the other hand, the plant outside was exposed to storms, strong winds, and the scorching sun. Each time it faced those challenges, it grew a little stronger. Its roots spread deep into the ground to anchor itself during storms, and its branches reached for the sunlight. Every challenge it faced made it tougher, and today, it stands tall and strong."

He continued, "Remember this lesson in your life, dear. If you choose the path of comfort, you may grow, but only within limits. But if you're willing to face life's challenges, to weather the storms and hardships, you will grow stronger than you ever imagined. Obstacles may seem like enemies at first, but they are opportunities in disguise—chances to grow, learn, and succeed."

The girl took a deep breath, staring at the mighty tree. She finally understood her grandfather's words. The obstacles she feared weren't enemies—they were what had made the tree so strong and successful. And just like that tree, she could grow stronger by facing the challenges ahead, rather than shying away from them.

The story of the girl and her grandfather illustrates a timeless truth: the greatest growth often comes from the greatest challenges. Just like the tree that grew stronger with every storm, we, too, develop resilience, strength, and wisdom by facing obstacles head-on.

Many people believe that success comes from avoiding difficulties, but the reality is quite the opposite. Obstacles force us out of our comfort zones, compelling us to think creatively, work harder, and develop skills we didn't even know we had. They shape us into stronger, more capable versions of ourselves, preparing us for even bigger challenges in the future.

When you shape your own path, as mentioned in this chapter, expect to face difficulties. These are not barriers to your success but building blocks of it. Every hurdle you overcome adds to your strength, and the more you persevere, the stronger your foundation becomes.

Another significant point in the story is the freedom the tree had to spread its roots and grow in the backyard. When we allow ourselves to embrace challenges and uncertainties, we give ourselves the freedom to explore our full potential. Staying inside a bubble of safety may seem appealing at first, but it limits growth. Real growth requires the freedom to stretch beyond limitations and explore the unknown.

In life, this means being open to new experiences, learning from failures, and taking calculated risks. When we are not afraid to step outside our comfort zones, we open the door to endless possibilities. We gain the freedom to create our own path, just like the tree spreading its roots far and wide.

The process of shaping your path is not without its difficulties. Life will throw storms at you—difficult decisions, setbacks, failures, and even moments of doubt. But like the tree growing stronger in the face of adversity, you too will become stronger with each challenge you face.

The real question is not whether you will face obstacles but how you will handle them. Will you let them break you, or will you use them as opportunities to learn and grow? Each obstacle you overcome is like a storm weathered by the tree, making your foundation even more solid.

Success doesn't come from avoiding hardship; it comes from persevering through it. The strongest individuals are those who have faced difficulties and come out stronger on the other side. They are like the tree that survived the storms and now stands tall, providing shelter and inspiration to others.

The story of the girl and her grandfather reminds us that facing challenges is not something to be feared, but something to be embraced. Just like the tree that grew strong in the backyard, we grow stronger when we step outside our comfort zones and face life's difficulties head-on.

When you shape your path, expect to face obstacles. They are not the enemies of your success but the very things that make success possible. Every storm you face strengthens your roots, deepening your foundation and preparing you for the future.

Obstacles and challenges are inevitable in life, but they play a critical role in shaping who we become. Often, we feel overwhelmed, discouraged, and sometimes even alone, as if no one else is experiencing the weight of our struggles. But in reality, everyone faces difficulties at various stages of their journey. How you deal with those challenges, however, is what ultimately determines your path.

Take a moment to reflect on the moments when you were lost, when problems seemed insurmountable. You likely thought at that time that the challenge in front of you was one of the hardest things you'd ever have to face. But here you are, on the other side, having overcome it. What may have felt impossible before now seems small in hindsight.

"I know that everyone faces challenges and obstacles in life where you feel so alone, depressed, and demotivated. At this time, what you need most is the willpower to get over the challenge. You and I both know that you will figure it out eventually. But what is required at that moment is patience and a working mindset. Often, we lose these, feel hopeless, and don't see a way out."

In those dark moments, just remember that you've faced similar situations before. Maybe those challenges seem trivial now, but at the time, they felt just as daunting. Yet, you still managed to find a way through them. Don't hesitate or doubt yourself. You have the capability, you just need to calm your mind and focus on solving the problem in front of you.

There is no challenge too big or too complicated that cannot be figured out. What you need is patience, hope, and a calm mindset. If you hold onto these principles, you will be able to navigate any challenge. Take a deep breath and realize that the obstacle in front of you is just another opportunity for growth.

In the heat of the moment, when life feels overwhelming and the challenges seem endless, it's easy to lose perspective. It's natural to feel demotivated, but this is the time to remind yourself that every problem has a solution. You've solved problems before, and you will solve them again.

What often separates success from failure is the ability to stay calm under pressure. When you let anxiety or fear take over, you lose the clarity needed to navigate challenges. Instead, if you approach each problem with a calm mind and the knowledge that every challenge is an opportunity for growth, you set yourself up for success.

Many people give up not because the challenge is too big, but because they are too focused on the problem instead of looking for solutions. The mindset with which you approach a problem matters as much as the problem itself. If you can maintain hope and practice patience, the solution will reveal itself in time.

A Practical Strategy for Problem Solving

1. Acknowledge the Challenge: The first step to overcoming any obstacle is recognizing it. Don't shy away from it or deny its presence. Acknowledge that there's a challenge in front of you, and that it's something you need to deal with.
2. Stay Calm: When faced with challenges, we often let emotions like frustration or anxiety cloud our judgment. Before attempting to solve the problem, take a step back, breathe, and center yourself. A calm mind leads to clearer thoughts.
3. Recall Past Successes: When you feel demotivated, remind yourself of the obstacles you've already overcome in life. What seemed overwhelming in the past is likely insignificant today. This will remind you that you're capable of overcoming anything, as long as you stay persistent.
4. Break the Problem Down: Sometimes a challenge feels massive because we see it as one big problem. Break it down into smaller, more manageable parts. This not only makes it easier to solve but also gives you small wins along the way, boosting your

motivation.

5. Seek Solutions, Not Excuses: Focus on how to resolve the issue rather than dwelling on why it's difficult. Obstacles are not meant to halt progress, but to teach us valuable lessons. Every challenge you face can be a learning experience if you allow it to be.
6. Maintain Hope: Lastly, no matter how difficult things may seem, always hold onto hope. Believing that there is a way out, even if you can't see it right now, is critical to maintaining the energy and mindset needed to overcome the challenge.

Challenges Shape Your Path. It's important to realize that challenges don't just test us—they shape us. The same way that plants grow stronger and more resilient when exposed to harsh conditions, we too grow tougher and more capable when we face adversity. The road to success is rarely smooth. It's filled with setbacks, unexpected turns, and obstacles. But these are not roadblocks—they are stepping stones. Every challenge is an opportunity to learn, grow, and become better.

When we look at successful people, it's easy to admire their accomplishments, but we often overlook the obstacles they had to overcome to get there. It's not the absence of challenges that leads to success; it's the ability to navigate them that makes the difference.

Your path to success will have its share of difficulties, but that's what will make your journey unique and rewarding. Obstacles are not there to prevent you from succeeding; they are there to prepare you for success. Every challenge you face teaches you something new, and the more you learn, the more capable you become of handling future challenges.Life is filled with challenges, but it's how you respond to those challenges that will shape your path to success. Obstacles may seem like roadblocks at first, but they are actually the tools that help you grow stronger and more resilient.Just like the plant that grows stronger by facing the elements, you too will grow stronger when you face your challenges head-on. By embracing patience, staying calm, and approaching problems with a mindset focused on solutions, you can turn any challenge into an opportunity for growth.

Why worry about challenges when they are the very things that will make you stronger?

CHAPTER V

# Why to Worry When Learning Fuels Success

One of the most fundamental aspects of achieving success is cultivating a growth mindset—a belief that abilities and intelligence can be developed through dedication, effort, and learning. Unlike a fixed mindset, where individuals think their talents are static and unchangeable, a growth mindset encourages an ongoing journey of improvement. It is the understanding that failure is not a reflection of your limitations but an opportunity to learn, evolve, and eventually excel.

When you adopt a growth mindset, challenges no longer feel like roadblocks but stepping stones. Instead of avoiding difficult tasks, a growth mindset drives you to take them on, understanding that they provide the most valuable learning experiences. Each challenge, no matter how daunting, is an opportunity to develop new skills and improve existing ones. This shift in perspective is empowering—because when you stop fearing failure, you're more willing to venture out of your comfort zone and push your boundaries.

For example, consider how the mindset shapes your approach to professional growth. Imagine you're assigned a project that requires skills you're not confident in. Someone with a fixed mindset might feel overwhelmed and hesitant, fearing they'll fail and expose their weaknesses. But someone with a growth mindset sees the task as a chance to learn something new. They approach it with curiosity, determination, and the understanding that even if they stumble along the way, they'll come out stronger for it.

A growth mindset fosters resilience. When faced with setbacks or failures, a person with this mindset doesn't give up easily. Instead, they persist, knowing that success often comes through perseverance. It's about viewing effort as a necessary part of the process rather than a sign that you're not good enough. You understand that with time and commitment, you'll get better at whatever you're pursuing.

The journey of successful entrepreneurs, artists, athletes, and leaders illustrates this point. They didn't succeed because they were born with extraordinary talent—they succeeded because they continually honed their skills, learned from failures, and adapted. The belief in their ability to improve kept them going when others would have given up.

Another vital aspect of a growth mindset is the ability to learn from feedback."Learning from Criticism". Instead of viewing criticism as an attack on your abilities, you begin to see it as valuable information that can help you grow. Constructive criticism offers insights into areas where you can improve, and rather than feeling defensive, you embrace it as part of your development.

This mindset also opens the door to collaboration. When you're secure in the belief that you can improve, you're more open to listening to others, taking their advice, and implementing it in ways that enhance your skills and knowledge. In professional environments, the growth mindset turns teamwork into a richer experience where feedback is welcomed rather than feared.

The key to understanding the power of a growth mindset is realizing that success is not a static goal—it's a continuous journey. No matter where you are, there is always room for improvement. When you stop seeing your abilities as fixed, you allow yourself to embrace the learning process. Whether you're working on personal development, relationships, or career growth, this mindset keeps you striving for better.

The famous psychologist Carol Dweck, who coined the concept of a growth mindset, highlighted how even the most talented individuals remain students of their craft throughout their lives. They recognize that learning never stops. That's why the most successful people in any field constantly seek to refine their skills, expand their knowledge, and better themselves.

A growth mindset reinforces the belief that effort is what leads to mastery. While talent or intelligence may give you a head start, it's sustained effort that brings long-term success. The most accomplished musicians, athletes, and innovators didn't get to where they are by coasting on natural ability alone. They invested countless hours into practice, experimentation, and learning from their mistakes.

As you apply this mindset to your life, you'll realize that effort isn't something to avoid or resent. It's the very thing that will take you from where you are now to where you want to be. The effort you put in today will compound over time, leading to results far greater than you might expect.Cultivating a growth mindset allows you to see potential where others see limits. By embracing challenges, persisting through difficulties, learning from feedback, and committing to continuous improvement, you create a pathway to success that never ends. With a growth mindset, there are no failures—only lessons. Each day brings new opportunities to learn, grow, and move closer to your goals.This mindset is the foundation of lifelong learning and the fuel that will propel you forward, no matter what obstacles you face.

So, why worry about where you are today, when you know that with the right mindset, tomorrow holds even greater possibilities?

Life is constantly changing. Whether it's shifts in your personal life, career transitions, or even global events, one thing is certain—change is inevitable. How we adapt to these changes can often determine our level of success and happiness. A growth mindset not only embraces challenges but also welcome growth.

Adaptability is one of the most important skills anyone can develop. It's the ability to adjust your mindset, habits, and actions when circumstances change. Instead of resisting or fearing the unknown, adaptable people see change as an opportunity to evolve, learn, and make progress.

Consider the year 2020, when the COVID-19 pandemic suddenly changed the way we live, work, and interact. People and organizations around the world had to quickly adjust to new norms. Remote working, digital meetings, and online learning became the standard, forcing everyone to develop new skills, find new ways to be productive, and adapt to an uncertain future. Those who were flexible and open to learning new methods not only survived this period but thrived.

Take businesses, for example. Many restaurants that initially relied on in-person dining had to shift to online delivery and curbside pick-up to stay afloat. The ones that adapted quickly managed to navigate the crisis, while those resistant to change struggled. This period demonstrated that being open to adaptation is often the difference between success and failure, especially in rapidly evolving environments.

Adapting to change doesn't always have to be monumental. Sometimes, it's in the smaller moments that adaptation truly matters. Take learning new technology, for example. As software and tools constantly evolve, workers in nearly every industry need to learn new platforms and techniques to stay relevant. Those who adapt by embracing lifelong learning stay ahead, while those who resist often find themselves falling behind.

Similarly, in your personal life, adapting to changing circumstances—whether moving to a new city, entering a new relationship, or starting a new job—can help you grow and thrive. It's not about fearing what's ahead but seeing change as an opportunity to explore new possibilities. At the heart of adaptability is the growth mindset. When you see challenges and changes as learning experiences, you're more likely to handle them with grace and resilience. Instead of asking, "Why is this happening to me?" a person with a growth mindset asks, "What can I learn from this?" That simple shift in perspective opens up countless opportunities for growth.

In today's fast-paced world, adaptability has become an invaluable trait in the job market. With technology evolving rapidly and industries undergoing constant transformation, those who can quickly adjust and learn new skills are the ones who rise to the top. For example, in the tech industry, programming languages and tools change frequently. Software developers need to stay current with new languages, frameworks, and methodologies to remain competitive.

Even in industries like education, adaptability has become crucial. With the rise of e-learning and virtual classrooms, educators had to swiftly adapt their teaching methods to engage students online. Teachers who embraced the change learned new platforms, found creative ways to connect with students, and continued to thrive in this new digital environment.

In a broader sense, adapting to change helps you build resilience. Life is full of unexpected twists and turns. The more flexible you are in facing these changes, the more successful and fulfilled you'll become.

So, why worry about change when it's often the very thing that will lead you to success?

Failure is often seen as something to be avoided at all costs, but in reality, it is one of the most valuable teachers in life. Every failure presents a unique opportunity to grow, reflect, and learn. When we experience setbacks, it forces us to re-evaluate our approach, analyze our mistakes, and ultimately become better versions of ourselves. Failure gives us the chance to pause and reflect, helping us understand what went wrong and how we can avoid repeating the same mistakes in the future.

Think about successful innovators, athletes, and entrepreneurs—their paths are paved with countless failures. What sets them apart is not the absence of failure, but their ability to learn from it and use it as fuel to push forward. Each misstep becomes a stepping stone toward eventual success. Instead of seeing failure as the end of the road, embrace it as part of the learning process.

Failure also builds resilience. When things don't go as planned, we develop the mental toughness to face future challenges with more grit and determination. The key is to shift your perspective: rather than viewing failure as a setback, see it as an opportunity to learn, grow, and improve. With every failed attempt, you are one step closer to success. As the saying goes, "Failing is not falling down, but refusing to get up." It is in these moments of defeat that we are presented with the greatest opportunities to evolve.

Success is not a fixed point you reach and then stop. It's a continuous journey of growth, exploration, and evolution. The moment we believe we have nothing more to learn is the moment we stop progressing. Lifelong learning is the key to achieving sustained success because it keeps us open to new possibilities, ideas, and improvements. Every experience, whether good or bad, offers an opportunity to learn something new. When you adopt the mindset of always being a student of life, you embrace curiosity, creativity, and adaptability.

Staying open to learning ensures that you continue to evolve and remain relevant in a constantly changing world. Whether it's learning a new skill, understanding a different perspective, or mastering a subject, the habit of lifelong learning enriches your life and strengthens your ability to overcome challenges. Success, then, is not about reaching a final destination but about becoming a better version of yourself every day. Lifelong learners keep their minds sharp and their potential limitless. By continuing to grow, they fuel their success with each step, embracing the idea that every day presents an opportunity to learn something new.

To foster a lifelong learning mindset, it's essential to integrate learning into your daily life with practical, actionable strategies. First, start by setting clear goals for what you want to learn. Whether it's mastering a new skill, diving into a subject area, or improving your personal development, having specific goals gives you direction. Create small, manageable learning targets to keep yourself on track.Finding a mentor is another valuable step. Learning from someone who has already walked the path you are on can provide insights and guidance, helping you avoid mistakes and accelerate your growth. Mentors offer a wealth of experience and can give you personalized advice based on their own journeys.

Reading books is one of the most powerful and accessible ways to learn. From self-improvement to biographies, reading broadens your perspective and deepens your knowledge in countless areas. In today's digital world, taking online courses is another great way to enhance your learning. Platforms like Coursera, Udemy, and

LinkedIn Learning offer endless resources for expanding your skills in both professional and personal domains.

Finally, it's essential to apply what you learn. Knowledge without action is ineffective. Whether it's a new skill or an insight you've gained, actively integrating what you've learned into your daily life cements it into your routine. By setting goals, finding mentors, reading, taking courses, and applying your knowledge, you can enhance your learning and continuously grow in ways that fuel your long-term success.

CHAPTER VI

# Why to Worry When You Can Control Your Mind

Anxiety is something most of us have faced at some point, whether it's a looming deadline, a difficult conversation, or even just the many "what-ifs" we carry about the future. Our minds, if left unchecked, can become like runaway trains, speeding towards all kinds of worst-case scenarios. But what if we could learn to control our minds and steer that train in the direction we want?

The truth is, our thoughts hold an immense amount of power over our emotions. If our mind dwells on fears and anxieties, we're likely to feel overwhelmed and stuck. However, if we train ourselves to recognize these thoughts and guide them toward calmer, more positive places, we start to regain control.

Imagine your mind as a garden. When we let anxiety grow, it's like allowing weeds to spread unchecked. It doesn't take long before they crowd out the healthy, positive plants. But with practice, we can pull out those weeds—those anxious thoughts—and choose to nurture thoughts that bring us peace and strength instead.

Anxiety often brings sleepless nights, a whirlwind of thoughts about career pressures, social expectations, or what others think of us. It can be an all-consuming worry, making it difficult to move forward. I remember a time when a deeply emotional event sent me spiraling into overthinking. Nights became challenging, filled with tears, shaky breaths, and hands trembling from an overload of anxious thoughts. I felt trapped, wondering if I'd ever regain peace. But over time, I learned that although I couldn't control the flow of thoughts entering my mind, I could definitely control how I deal with them.

Through patience and practice, I found ways to decide whether each thought was worth my time and energy. Was it really necessary to dwell on? Did it serve any purpose other than to exhaust me? Recognizing that I had the choice over which thoughts to entertain allowed me to find a new level of inner calm.

Each time we face anxiety, we have the opportunity to pause, breathe, and decide our next step. We can choose not to engage with every worry or fear that comes our way, learning instead to let those thoughts float by like clouds. With patience and persistence, we can transform our minds from gardens overrun by weeds to spaces of peace and resilience.

Remember, it's not about stopping anxious thoughts altogether; it's about deciding which ones are worth holding onto. And each time we choose to let go of what doesn't serve us, we reclaim a little more peace.

Ever found yourself lying awake late at night, overwhelmed by thoughts that seem to have no end? Questions like: Why did that happen to me? What did I do wrong? Why did certain people come into my life only to leave when I needed them the most? Why am I even here? It's as if your mind is filled with endless question marks, each one more puzzling than the last.

So yes to all the thoughts filled with question marks??? remember If there are no answers, there's a reason. Sometimes, life doesn't hand us answers immediately because it wants us to focus on the journey, not just the solution. These unanswered questions can feel heavy, but they often guide us toward growth, self-discovery, and ultimately, a deeper understanding of ourselves and the world around us.

The first step in controlling anxiety is awareness. When a worried thought creeps in, try to notice it instead of getting swept away. It's like standing on the edge of a river and watching leaves float by—just because you see a thought doesn't mean you have to jump in and follow it down the stream. When you spot an anxious thought, acknowledge it, and try to understand its source. Why are you feeling this way? Is the fear real, or is it just a habit of overthinking?

Once you recognize these thoughts, practice redirecting them. Instead of “What if I fail?” try “What if I succeed?” Changing our perspective on things that worry us can have an enormous impact on our mental state.Try to think positively and stop regretting things. The best way I deal with it is by considering myself lucky.

The concept of luck often feels intangible—something beyond our control. But is it? Research and experiments suggest that luck is more about perspective, mindset, and approach than mere coincidence. Psychologist Dr. Richard Wiseman conducted an interesting study to explore what makes someone "lucky" or "unlucky," and the results are fascinating.

Dr. Richard Wiseman conducted a fascinating experiment to understand the mindset of "lucky" versus "unlucky" people. He gave participants a newspaper and asked them to count the number of photographs inside.

On average, the unlucky participants took about two minutes to count the photographs, while the lucky participants completed the task in mere seconds. The reason? On the second page of the newspaper, there was a large message that read, “Stop counting — There are 43 photographs in this newspaper.” This message occupied half the page and was printed in bold letters over two inches high—impossible to miss. Yet, the unlucky participants often overlooked it, while the lucky participants spotted it almost immediately.

To take the experiment further, Wiseman added another large message halfway through the newspaper. This one read, “Stop counting, tell the experimenter you have seen this and win $250.” Once again, the lucky participants noticed and took advantage of this opportunity, while the unlucky ones missed it because they were too focused on counting photographs.

This experiment demonstrates that luck often comes down to perspective and mindset. Lucky people tend to be more relaxed and open to unexpected opportunities, while unlucky people, due to their focus or stress, may overlook what’s right in front of them. It’s a powerful reminder that being alert, adaptable, and optimistic can help you spot opportunities that others might miss.Wiseman's research also revealed an intriguing aspect of luck: people who feel lucky often believe they have control over their lives, even in unpredictable situations. This sense of control empowers them to make the best of their circumstances, turning challenges into opportunities. On the other hand, those who feel unlucky often give away their power, believing that external factors solely dictate their fate.

Believing in luck is, in essence, a form of manifestation. When we consider ourselves lucky, we unconsciously act in ways that align with that belief. We stay more alert, are willing to take risks, and are open to opportunities. This mindset creates a self-fulfilling cycle, where the belief in luck leads to actions that invite fortunate outcomes.Conversely, people who label themselves as unlucky often operate from a place of fear and anxiety. They focus on what could go wrong, miss cues in their environment, and inadvertently reinforce their belief in bad luck. For instance, in the experiment, their rushed approach to finding the words caused them to miss what was right in front of them.

Cultivating a "lucky" mindset begins with staying observant. Like the newspaper experiment demonstrated, opportunities are often hidden in plain sight, waiting for us to notice them. Being positive is equally crucial—shifting your thoughts from "What if I fail?" to "What if I succeed?" can transform your outlook, opening doors to success and new possibilities. Luck also favors those who take calculated risks, stepping out of their comfort zones to try something new or embrace challenges, which increases the chances of encountering unexpected opportunities. Moreover, creating opportunities for yourself is key; luck isn't just about waiting for things to happen but actively making them happen by networking, learning new skills, and seeking out enriching experiences. Lastly, believing in your own luck can be a game-changer. When you consider yourself lucky, you tend to act with confidence and calmness, attracting positive outcomes and reinforcing your sense of control over life's uncertainties.

Anxiety often causes our body to tense up and our breathing to become shallow, which, in turn, makes us feel even more anxious. Simple breathing exercises can help counteract this. Try taking a few slow, deep breaths whenever you feel anxious. Inhale for four seconds, hold for four, and exhale for four. This type of breathing not only calms your nervous system but also distracts your mind from anxious thoughts, bringing you back to the present moment.

Visualization is another powerful tool. When anxious, try to picture yourself in a calm, confident state. Imagine yourself handling the situation successfully. Whether it's a presentation, an interview, or a social event, picture yourself doing well. This practice reinforces positive beliefs and prepares your mind to face challenges without unnecessary fear.

One of the biggest culprits of anxiety is our mind's tendency to worry about the future. Practicing mindfulness—focusing on the present moment—can help reduce this tendency. Try paying attention to small, sensory details around you: the sound of birds, the taste of your food, or the feel of a soft blanket. By bringing your attention to the present, you reduce your mind's ability to drift into anxious thoughts about what could go wrong.Another effective way to ease anxiety is by engaging in activities you love. Whether it's reading books, dancing, drawing, or journaling your thoughts, these pursuits can offer an emotional release and a sense of calm. Writing down the things you can't share with anyone can be particularly therapeutic. Alternatively, confiding in someone you trust can lighten the mental burden—choose someone who respects your vulnerability.

When anxiety strikes, it's easy to get down on ourselves, to feel as though we should be stronger or that something is wrong with us. But remember that anxiety is a normal human experience. Practicing self-compassion can be transformative. Remind yourself that it's okay to feel anxious and that you're taking steps to manage it. Treat yourself kindly and encourage yourself like you would a friend. The more you accept and support yourself, the more you'll be able to control your reactions to anxiety.

Learning to control your mind is a gradual process. There may be days when anxiety feels overwhelming, but know that each step you take toward managing your thoughts brings you closer to a place of peace. Change doesn't happen overnight, and the journey is just as important as the destination.

By cultivating awareness, practicing mindfulness, and allowing yourself grace, you'll start seeing how much power you have over your own mind. You'll discover that worry no longer holds you back. Instead, your mind becomes an ally, ready to face life's challenges with calm, confidence, and resilience.

After all, why worry when you can control your mind?

CHAPTER VII

# Why to Worry When Time is Your Ally

We often think of time as something that slips away, a limited resource that must be carefully managed, or a ticking clock that pressures us to hurry. But what if we could see time as our friend, not our foe? What if, instead of chasing or fearing it, we trusted that time is here to guide and support us? Embracing this perspective can transform how we experience life, turning anxiety about deadlines, milestones, or the future into peace and patience. After all, time, when harnessed well, becomes our greatest ally in learning, healing, and achieving what truly matters.

Time offers us a unique opportunity to learn from experiences, whether they're successes or missteps. Think about any skill or subject you've pursued. Whether it's a sport, a craft, or a course, time has likely helped you refine and grow. Even the mistakes along the way served as stepping stones, teaching you valuable lessons you couldn't learn otherwise. Each effort, regardless of the result, adds to a foundation that time alone helps to build.

Consider the journey of a tree. It doesn't grow overnight; it needs time to root deeply, to reach up to the sun, and to bear fruit. Rushing the process could only harm it, but given enough time, it grows strong and resilient. In a similar way, time patiently shapes and supports us, even when we don't see it. Every moment—every lesson, every encounter—is like a ring in the tree's trunk, a silent but powerful indicator of growth and resilience.

Time also plays a remarkable role in healing. When we face setbacks, disappointment, or loss, it's natural to feel weighed down by pain. But as days go by, time has a way of lightening that burden. With each passing moment, our minds and hearts process these feelings, allowing wounds to heal, slowly but surely. By simply allowing ourselves to feel, process, and eventually release, time gently helps us move forward.

Think back to a time in your own life when you faced a challenging setback. Initially, it might have seemed impossible to get past it. But gradually, as days turned into weeks and weeks into months, you probably found a way forward. The pain lessened, and new opportunities or perspectives appeared. This doesn't mean we forget our struggles; instead, it demonstrates time's extraordinary ability to soften pain and build resilience.

Healing isn't just about getting over a tough breakup (though yes, time helps with that, too!). It could be bouncing back from a failure or facing an unexpected challenge. We often feel like we're trapped in a loop with no way out, but as time goes on, things fall into place, and we learn to cope.

Everything needs time, and time itself is essential for healing. Remember, each difficult moment will eventually pass, allowing us to come out stronger and more prepared for whatever lies ahead.

Time management is one of those skills that feels harder and harder to master as we transition into adulthood. Waking up at 7:00 a.m., which seemed effortless in our school days, now feels like an impossible feat. Remember those early mornings when getting out of bed, showering, and getting ready was routine? Fast forward to now, and hitting snooze until the last possible second seems more familiar. Many of us know the frustration of wanting to be productive, but we're held back by a lack of structure—sometimes, it's our sleep schedule, and other times, it's simply the pull of endless distractions.

At some point, nearly everyone has tried the "time management reboot." You might have put up a colorful time-table on your wall or downloaded a time management app to help organize your day. Maybe you watched motivational videos or meticulously planned out every hour of your week. It probably felt empowering, and maybe it even worked for a few days. But then, life happened, distractions crept in, and eventually, those well-laid plans fizzled out.

This struggle—wanting to be productive but feeling overwhelmed by poor time management—is more common than we admit. Fixing sleep schedules and forming a routine often feel like an uphill battle. Even though we all have the potential to be more productive, our days slip by in a haze of missed schedules, and we lose a bit of motivation each time it happens.

Yet, here's the truth: time management isn't about rigidly following a strict plan or perfectly controlling every minute. It's more about balance and learning to respect your own energy and focus levels. Yes, there will be days when we fall short, but by showing ourselves a bit of grace and understanding, we can begin to build routines that suit our lives, not restrict them. So, the next time you're tempted to start from scratch with a new "perfect" schedule, remember that consistency, rather than perfection, is the real key to making time work in your favor.

Each phase of life, each change, and each experience brings valuable lessons that only time can reveal. When we're young, there's often a rush to accomplish, experience, and prove ourselves immediately. Yet, some of the most important things in life only come into focus with time. As we grow, we start to understand that patience and persistence often lead to far greater rewards than the rush of immediate satisfaction.

Think about something like a smartwatch or gadget you once desperately wanted, the one you might have begged your parents for, convinced it was essential. Now, it's probably lying around somewhere, uncharged and forgotten. There was a time when you wore it constantly, feeling it was the ultimate accessory. Getting the newest watch or bike once felt thrilling and necessary, yet as time passes, we start seeing these desires in a new light. Time has a way of teaching us to appreciate things at their true worth, beyond the initial excitement.

Time also teaches us that everything has its own season. The dreams we pursue, the relationships we build, and the projects we undertake all grow at their own pace. Often, when we reflect on our journey, we realize that certain experiences—whether joyous or challenging—were necessary to prepare us for what was next. Every phase, every chapter of life, is woven together in a way that only time could design, guiding us and helping us grow in the way we're meant to.

It's easy to worry when things don't happen as quickly as we expect. Maybe it's a delayed goal or an opportunity that feels just out of reach. But if we can remind ourselves that time has its own rhythm, we can find a sense of calm and trust that everything will fall into place when it's meant to. Like a river flowing naturally, time moves us forward even when we think we're standing still.

Trusting in time's timing can be one of life's greatest reliefs. Instead of resisting, pushing, or forcing things to happen, we can let go, knowing that time is guiding us. By accepting this flow, we may find that things come together in ways we couldn't have anticipated, often in the perfect moment.

Why to Worry When Time Is On Your Side

Ultimately, time is not here to rush us or to hold us back. It's here to teach, heal, and support us in becoming the best version of ourselves. With every passing day, we grow closer to our goals, more prepared for our future, and more resilient in the face of challenges.

So, the next time you feel anxious or impatient, remember: time is your ally, not your enemy. Let go of the rush, trust in the journey, and know that with patience, persistence, and faith, time will guide you to where you're meant to be. Embrace each moment fully, knowing that it's helping you grow, step by step, into the person you're destined to become.

CHAPTER VIII

# Why to Worry When Responsibility Unlocks Potential

Responsibility is often seen as a burden, something that weighs us down or takes away our freedom. But what if we shifted our perspective? What if we looked at responsibility not as something that confines us but as an opportunity to unlock our true potential?

Every responsibility we take on challenges us in unique ways. It pushes us out of our comfort zones, forcing us to learn, adapt, and grow. Think of the first time you were trusted with something significant—a school project, managing a task at work, or even taking care of someone. At first, it might have felt overwhelming, but over time, you probably realized that you were capable of much more than you initially thought. Responsibility helps us discover strengths we never knew we had.

Responsibility is about demonstrating that you are capable and dependable. Have you ever been assigned a task with a deadline and, instead of pacing yourself, waited until the last moment to start working on it? The overwhelming pressure kicks in, and you somehow manage to complete the task just in time. I used to follow this same unproductive habit, rushing through tasks simply to meet the deadline.

However, over time, I realized that while I was capable of finishing the work, the quality often fell short of what I could truly achieve. Instead of showcasing my full potential, I was merely completing tasks for the sake of it. By approaching responsibilities with proper planning and focus, I began to deliver work that not only met expectations but exceeded them, proving that I was reliable and worthy of trust. Responsibility isn't just about finishing a job—it's about doing it thoughtfully, effectively, and in a way that highlights your true potential.

When we take on responsibility, we also learn the value of accountability. Being accountable means owning our actions and decisions, whether they lead to success or failure. This sense of ownership builds confidence and resilience, as it empowers us to learn from our experiences and adapt. It's a powerful realization: while we may not control everything that happens to us, we do control how we respond.

Consider this example: imagine a young professional tasked with leading their first project at work. Initially, they are excited, but as the project progresses, unforeseen challenges arise. Deadlines slip, team coordination falters, and a critical client presentation doesn't go as planned. It's tempting to blame external factors—tight schedules, uncooperative team members, or even bad luck. But instead of pointing fingers, this individual takes full responsibility.

They review what went wrong, own their mistakes, and approach their manager with a plan for improvement. They set clearer expectations for the team, establish better communication channels, and prioritize time management. With each step, they not only salvage the project but gain the respect of their peers and leadership.

This experience transforms their perspective. They realize that accountability is not about perfection—it's about growth. By owning the situation, they turn a challenging moment into a learning opportunity. Over time, this approach builds their confidence, making them more capable of handling responsibilities and navigating setbacks. Taking ownership isn't always easy, but it's what enables us to rise stronger and more prepared for the future.

Another beautiful aspect of responsibility is the trust that accompanies it. When someone entrusts us with a task, a role, or a duty, they are expressing their confidence in our abilities, integrity, and commitment to deliver. This trust is a silent yet powerful vote of faith that can serve as a profound motivator. It's more than an obligation; it's an acknowledgment of our potential, a recognition that we are capable of achieving something meaningful.

This trust inspires us to rise to the occasion. It pushes us to dig deeper, to channel our focus, and to deliver results that justify the faith placed in us. It serves as a mirror reflecting our own capabilities, reminding us of our strengths and encouraging us to overcome doubts or fears. The sense of accountability that comes with such trust often brings out our best qualities—discipline, determination, and resilience.

With every responsibility we fulfill, the trust placed in us grows stronger. It becomes a bridge to greater opportunities, fostering relationships built on mutual respect and reliability. Trust is not just a byproduct of responsibility; it is the very foundation that opens doors to leadership, collaboration, and growth. It allows us to contribute meaningfully to the lives of others, strengthening bonds and creating a ripple effect of positivity and progress.

In essence, responsibility is not just about completing tasks or meeting expectations. It is about honoring the trust that others place in us and proving, time and again, that we are worthy of it. It's a journey of self-discovery, a path to greater self-assurance, and a powerful tool to shape a life filled with purpose, achievement, and deep, meaningful connections.

Taking responsibility also teaches independence. It empowers us to make decisions, solve problems, and navigate challenges on our own. This independence is crucial for personal growth, as it enables us to rely less on others and trust more in our abilities. The confidence gained through responsible actions lays the foundation for a stronger, more self-assured version of ourselves.

From childhood, we've always dreamed of independence—freedom from restrictions, whether it's financial independence or the ability to make our own decisions. But with independence comes a cascade of responsibilities. As we grow older, these responsibilities naturally increase.

Think back to when we were children. Our parents, with unwavering dedication, sought the best schools for our education, often sacrificing their own comfort to ensure we had opportunities they may never have had. Over time, the roles begin to reverse.

One day, we'll find ourselves making decisions not only for our children—selecting their schools, supporting their dreams—but also for our parents, ensuring they receive the best medical care and attention in their later years. Responsibility becomes a bridge across generations, connecting us to those we love in meaningful ways.

For many, the moment they begin earning money is a turning point. At first, it feels liberating—a ticket to the freedom we always dreamed of. But soon, reality sets in. Alongside that paycheck come bills, obligations, and choices that may feel overwhelming. You may find yourself reflecting on the dreams you once had—visions of travel, passion projects, or personal achievements. Suddenly, those dreams seem distant, replaced by the immediate needs of loved ones and the circumstances life throws your way.

And yet, there's an unspoken beauty in this shift. Sacrifices made for the people we care about don't feel like burdens; they feel like acts of love. Without even realizing it, we compromise willingly, reshaping our dreams for the sake of others. These moments of selflessness, when viewed through the lens of responsibility, reveal our capacity to grow and adapt.

The key lies in embracing these responsibilities with strength and purpose. It's not just about managing what life demands—it's about proving to yourself, and to life itself, that "I am capable." Responsibilities don't diminish our independence; they enhance it by challenging us to rise to the occasion and become the best version of ourselves.

Yes, responsibility can feel daunting at times. There will be moments when the weight of expectations seems unbearable, when the pressure feels too much, or when things simply don't go as planned despite your best efforts. It's natural to feel overwhelmed, to doubt yourself, or even to wonder why the responsibility was given to you in the first place. However, it's important to remember that every responsibility you accept is a stepping stone toward unlocking your potential. It is not merely a task assigned to you—it's a significant opportunity to grow, to prove your worth, and to discover the strength you didn't realize you had.

Taking on responsibility requires courage. It means stepping out of your comfort zone and accepting challenges that might initially seem beyond your capabilities. Yet, it is within these moments of discomfort and uncertainty that true growth occurs. Each time you fulfill a responsibility, no matter how big or small, you build resilience. You learn to navigate obstacles, find creative solutions, and persevere even when the odds seem stacked against you. These experiences shape you into a stronger, more confident individual, capable of tackling even greater challenges in the future.

Responsibility is also an opportunity to showcase your abilities and prove your reliability to yourself and others. Each time you successfully manage a responsibility, you demonstrate that you are someone who can be trusted and depended upon. This trust, once earned, paves the way for new opportunities—be it in your career, relationships, or personal endeavors. With each responsibility, you are writing a story of capability and determination, one that inspires others and strengthens your belief in yourself.

At the same time, responsibility teaches us invaluable life skills—time management, prioritization, and the art of balancing multiple tasks. It pushes us to become more disciplined and organized, helping us to make better decisions and use our time effectively. These skills not only enable us to handle responsibilities better but also prepare us for future challenges that require even greater focus and dedication.

However, responsibility is not just about achieving outcomes; it's about embracing the journey. The lessons learned, the experiences gained, and the growth achieved along the way are far more valuable than the end result. Even when things don't go as planned, every effort you make is a testament to your commitment and willingness to rise to the occasion. Mistakes and setbacks are part of the process, and each one is an opportunity to learn and improve.

So, the next time life hands you a responsibility, don't shy away from it. Embrace it wholeheartedly, knowing that it's not just a task to complete but an opportunity to transform. Take it as a chance to uncover your hidden potential and realize your true capabilities. Remember that responsibility is not a burden—it's a gift, a path to self-discovery and growth. By shouldering responsibilities, you're not just meeting expectations; you're proving to yourself and the world that you are capable of achieving great things.

CHAPTER IX

# Why to Worry When Insecurities Drive Self-Improvement

Insecurities are often viewed as weaknesses—those little cracks in our confidence that we try to hide from the world. They can make us feel vulnerable, unworthy, or hesitant to pursue our goals. However, what if we told ourselves a different story?

This one goes out to those of us who woke up in a panic at 1 a.m. over how our hair looked on that Hinge date yesterday, the ones who are still semi-convinced they're very unqualified for their job, and those who cannot stop apologizing for existing. These are the victims of a ruthless criminal known as insecurity. Whether it's worrying about how you spoke to someone ("Did I say the right thing?"), obsessing over whether your outfit was right for the occasion ("Was I overdressed? Or worse, underdressed?"), or analyzing if your joke landed or just awkwardly hovered in the air like a balloon losing air—insecurities have a sneaky way of taking over.And let's not forget the universal nightmare: rethinking that one interaction from months ago. "Did I wave back awkwardly, or was it just in my head?" or "Why did I laugh so loudly at that joke?!" These thoughts spiral and convince us we've somehow failed. But here's the kicker: most people don't even remember these moments. The one who dwells on them is you. Why? Because you let someone else's fleeting comment or perceived judgment rent space in your head, costing you your peace of mind.The only one still holding onto it is you. Why let someone else's careless words ruin your sleep or mess with your mental peace? Seriously, get the hell out of that mindset. Those thoughts? They're not even worth a second of your precious time, dear. Let them go—you've got better things to do.

Instead of letting these thoughts haunt you, laugh at them, let them go, and remind yourself that even your so-called "cringe moments" are just tiny blips in the grand story of your life. Honestly, if someone remembers how you said "goodbye" awkwardly three years ago, that's their problem, not yours. Stop losing sleep over things that aren't even worth a second thought. Those thoughts? They're not your boss—you are.

Dealing with insecurities has always been a personal battle, but over time, I discovered my own way to face them—what I now call the Phoenix Principle. Like the mythical phoenix, I realized that every time I felt consumed by self-doubt or fear, it wasn't the end but an opportunity to rebuild and rise stronger. Instead of avoiding my insecurities, I acknowledged them, reflected on their root causes, and used them as a guide to areas where I could grow. I started small—celebrating little victories, practicing self-compassion, and learning to let go of past failures. Gradually, I began transforming my vulnerabilities into strengths, and every challenge became a stepping stone to personal growth. The Phoenix Principle has since been my guiding light, reminding me that every setback is a chance for renewal and that resilience is my greatest strength.

The Phoenix Principle draws inspiration from the mythical bird, the phoenix, a symbol of resilience, renewal, and transformation. According to legend, the phoenix is a magnificent creature that lives for centuries. When its life ends, it burns into ashes, only to rise again, reborn and stronger than before. The Phoenix Principle embodies this cycle of destruction and rebirth, teaching us that our insecurities, while challenging, hold the potential to transform us into stronger, more confident individuals.

Insecurities can feel overwhelming, like a fire consuming your confidence. They stem from various sources—self-doubt, past experiences, societal expectations, or fear of failure. But, just like the phoenix, these moments of vulnerability can ignite the spark for growth. The key lies in embracing insecurities as opportunities for self-discovery, renewal, and empowerment.

Applying the Phoenix Principle:

1. Acknowledge the Ashes

Before rising, the phoenix must turn to ashes, symbolizing the need to face and accept your insecurities. Avoiding or denying insecurities only gives them more power over you.Reflect on what triggers your feelings of inadequacy. Write them down to externalize these thoughts and gain clarity.Accept that insecurities are a natural part of being human. This is the first step toward transforming them.

2. Identify the Flames of Fear

Insecurities often thrive on fear—fear of judgment, failure, or rejection. By identifying these fears, you begin to diminish their power.Ask yourself, "What is the worst that can happen?" Often, the answers are far less catastrophic than they feel.Challenge irrational fears by focusing on evidence and past experiences where you overcame similar challenges.

3. Ignite Self-Belief

Rising from insecurities requires reigniting self-belief. Start by celebrating small wins and acknowledging your strengths.Create a "confidence journal" where you document accomplishments, no matter how small. This reinforces a positive self-image.Practice positive affirmations to replace self-doubt with empowering thoughts. For example, instead of saying, "I can't do this," tell yourself, "I am capable of learning and growing."

4. Rebuild with Intentional Growth

Use your insecurities as a guide to areas where growth is possible. If you feel insecure about a skill or trait, consider it an opportunity to improve.Invest in learning and development. Whether it's a new skill, public speaking, or fitness, small, consistent efforts create significant progress over time.Surround yourself with supportive people who encourage your growth rather than amplify your insecurities.

5. Rise with Gratitude and Perspective

Gratitude shifts the focus from what you lack to what you have. This mindset helps neutralize insecurities.Practice gratitude daily by listing three things you're thankful for. Gratitude fosters contentment and reduces the comparison trap.Gain perspective by reminding yourself that perfection doesn't exist. Even those you admire face their own insecurities.

6. Learn to Let Go of the Past

Just as the phoenix rises anew, you too can leave past failures and mistakes behind. They don't define your worth.Practice forgiveness—not only toward others but also yourself. Letting go of past regrets creates space for growth.Focus on what you can control in the present moment, rather than dwelling on what's already done.

7. Embrace Resilience as Your Superpower

The phoenix emerges stronger after every fall, a testament to resilience. Life will throw challenges your way, but each one prepares you for the next.Develop resilience by practicing self-care, setting healthy boundaries, and maintaining a balanced lifestyle.Remember, resilience isn't about never falling—it's about rising every time you do.

This strategy transforms insecurities into stepping stones for personal growth by fostering self-awareness, self-compassion, and a proactive mindset.Rather than fearing insecurities, view them as opportunities to reflect, grow, and rebuild. Every time you overcome an insecurity, you rise, more confident and capable than before. With the Phoenix Principle, you can transform the ashes of self-doubt into the flames of success and self-assurance.

Insecurities are a universal part of the human experience. They often stem from feelings of inadequacy, fear of failure, or comparison to others. While insecurities can feel overwhelming, they are also a mirror reflecting areas where we have room to grow. Instead of letting them hold us back, we can use our insecurities as catalysts for self-improvement.

One of the keys to turning insecurities into opportunities for self-improvement is self-awareness. The first step is identifying the root cause of your insecurity. Are you worried about your appearance? Your skills? Your relationships? Once you pinpoint the source, you can begin addressing it. Self-awareness allows you to shift from a mindset of self-criticism to one of self-compassion.

Another essential element is action. Improvement doesn't happen overnight, and it requires consistent effort. Start small by setting achievable goals related to your insecurities. If you feel insecure about a lack of knowledge in a certain area, commit to reading a book or taking a course. If your insecurity stems from physical fitness, begin with short workouts and gradually build a routine. Every step, no matter how small, brings you closer to overcoming that insecurity.

It's also crucial to surround yourself with positivity. Seek out supportive friends, mentors, or communities that encourage growth rather than magnify your doubts. Having people who believe in your potential can make a world of difference when you're working through insecurities.

Remember, insecurities are not weaknesses; they are challenges. Facing them head-on can teach you resilience, discipline, and courage. By embracing them as opportunities for self-improvement, you not only conquer your fears but also uncover hidden strengths.

So, the next time you feel the sting of insecurity, remind yourself: this is not a setback—it's a stepping stone. With the right mindset and effort, you can transform your insecurities into the foundation of a better, more confident you. Why worry, when even insecurities can drive you to become your best self?

To wrap it up, insecurities are like shadows—only noticeable when you let the light dim. Instead of letting them take center stage in your life, see them as signals for self-reflection and growth. Every time you feel insecure, pause and ask yourself, "What is this trying to teach me?" Then take action, even if it's a small step forward. And when those nagging thoughts creep in during the quiet hours, remind yourself that you're not defined by past moments or imagined judgments. You're the author of your own story, free to write a narrative of resilience and strength. Life is too precious to be lived in the confines of fear. So, embrace your quirks, stand unapologetically tall, and let the Phoenix Principle remind you that rising above is always an option. After all, isn't life meant to be a daring leap into self-belief?

CHAPTER X

# Why to Worry When Perfection is a Myth

Let's get one thing straight—perfection doesn't exist. It's a myth, a fantasy, a little lie we tell ourselves that we've somehow bought into over the years. We've all had that moment where we've re-watched a video we made or stared at a photo we posted, analyzing every tiny detail—"Oh, my smile was too big," "Did my laugh sound awkward?" or "Maybe I should have worn something else." The truth? Perfection is overrated, and the more we chase it, the more we find ourselves running in circles.

Perfection has a funny way of sneaking into our lives through social media, TV shows, and glossy magazine covers. But guess what? Those images aren't real. They're curated, edited, and filtered to fit a mold that's unattainable for anyone. What we're not seeing are the bloopers, the imperfect moments, and the behind-the-scenes struggles. You see, perfection isn't something to aim for—it's something that holds us back. It's the little voice in your head telling you that your best isn't enough, and it stops you from taking risks, from growing, and from showing up as your true self.

Think about it—if we were all perfect, would we really have anything to learn? Would we even know the feeling of accomplishment? Perfection removes the magic from trying, from failing, and from eventually getting it right. Success, growth, and real fulfillment come from embracing the messiness of life—the mistakes, the slip-ups, and yes, even the awkward moments. Those are the parts of life that make us human, and they're what shape us into the people we're meant to become.

So here's the deal—ditch the idea of perfection and embrace imperfection. Let's be real: Nobody's life is as flawless as it appears on the surface, and that's totally okay. What matters more is showing up, doing your best, and learning as you go. The next time you catch yourself aiming for perfection, ask yourself, "What's really more important here—doing it perfectly or doing it authentically?" You'll find that authenticity, not perfection, is where the true magic happens.

We live in a world where comparison is practically ingrained in our daily routines. From the moment we wake up and scroll through social media to the time we head to bed, we're constantly comparing ourselves to others. We measure our success against theirs, our appearance against theirs, and sometimes even our worth against theirs. But here's a truth that can't be overstated: no one is perfect, and everyone is unique in their own way.

Think about it—there's no one else exactly like you on this planet. Your style, your behavior, your quirks, and your habits are all what make you... well, YOU. The way you speak, the way you dress, the way you laugh, and the way you approach life—all these things make you a one-of-a-kind masterpiece. And that's something to celebrate. Perfection, as we know it, is a construct—a fleeting, ever-changing idea that society imposes upon us. Perfection is a moving target, one that, no matter how hard you try, will always feel out of reach. But uniqueness? That's yours to own.

In a world where social media often gives us curated glimpses into other people's lives, it's easy to think everyone else has it figured out while we're still stumbling through. You may find yourself wondering, "Why is their life so much better than mine?" or "Why do they seem to have it all together?" But the truth is, what you see is rarely the full picture. Behind every perfectly posed picture or every seemingly perfect success story, there are struggles, failures, and imperfections—things we don't often see because society has conditioned us to show only the best versions of ourselves.

When you start comparing yourself to others, you forget one essential fact: their journey is theirs and yours is yours. Everyone has their own timeline, their own pace, and their own way of doing things. Just because someone is ahead in one area doesn't mean you're failing. We all have different strengths and weaknesses, and comparing your behind-the-scenes to someone else's highlight reel is a recipe for disappointment. Instead of focusing on how you measure up to others, shift your focus to your own personal growth and uniqueness. What makes you different? What strengths do you bring to the table? These are the things that matter, and these are the things that will truly set you apart in a way that no amount of comparison ever could.

Consider how each person's style is a reflection of their personality. You might admire someone's impeccable fashion sense, but the truth is, that sense of style isn't about perfect clothes—it's about their confidence in wearing them. The most beautiful outfits are often those worn with authenticity, the ones that make you feel comfortable and confident. What works for one person might not work for you, and that's okay. The key is to embrace what works for you, whether it's that quirky style you love or those perfectly imperfect choices that define who you are. Your style is an extension of your personality—it's your way of saying, "This is me, and I'm proud of it."

The same applies to your behavior and habits. We all have our own unique ways of doing things, and those habits are part of what makes us different. You might be someone who thrives under pressure, or maybe you're more methodical and enjoy taking your time. Either way, there's no right or wrong. The key is to embrace who you are, without worrying about how others are doing things. Just because someone else is more outgoing or more introverted, more structured or more spontaneous, doesn't make them any more or less valuable than you. What makes you special is your individuality.

Take a moment to reflect on your own habits and behaviors. Are there things you do that others might not understand, but that make you feel comfortable and authentic? Embrace those habits. They're a reflection of your personal journey and growth. You don't need to follow someone else's script to be successful. You are successful when you stay true to who you are and trust that your path is just as valuable as anyone else's.

And this is where the magic happens: nothing can beat the real you. The most attractive quality a person can possess is authenticity. When you stop pretending to be someone you're not and start living as the real version of yourself, you exude confidence, self-respect, and an energy that draws people in. It's about owning your flaws, celebrating your strengths, and walking through life unapologetically yourself. When you live authentically, the comparisons fade away, and what remains is the most powerful thing you have—the true you.

But, let's be real for a second. It's easy to say, "Be yourself," but much harder to put into practice, especially when the pressure to conform feels overwhelming. We live in a society that loves to put people in boxes, label them, and dictate what success looks like. But let's break free of those expectations. The best part about not comparing yourself to others is that you finally realize you are enough—just as you are. The flaws, the quirks, the imperfections—they all make you who you are. It's time to stop running from them and start embracing them.

When you stop comparing yourself to others, you unlock a new sense of freedom. You no longer have to live up to anyone's standards but your own. You set your own goals, define your own success, and march to the beat of your own drum. Nothing can beat the real you because the real you is unshakable, unique, and irreplaceable.

So, stop worrying about how you measure up to others. Celebrate your individuality. Embrace your quirks, your style, your habits, and your uniqueness. They are what make you stand out, and that's something worth being proud of. When you start focusing on your own journey and stop comparing yourself to others, you'll discover that the only person you need to be better than is the person you were yesterday. You don't need to be perfect. You just need to be authentically you. And trust me, that's enough.

Stop stressing over those tiny flaws that no one notices. Stop replaying that awkward moment in your head for the thousandth time. Stop worrying about whether you're good enough or if you measure up to some imaginary standard. Because, in the grand scheme of things, none of that matters. Perfection is nothing but a distraction—a shiny illusion we use to avoid stepping outside our comfort zones, to avoid growth. It's a wall we build to keep ourselves from doing the very things that will help us move forward. The truth is, there's no such thing as perfect, and that's perfectly fine. In fact, it's more than fine. Perfection is overrated, and it's often the reason we stay stuck in places we don't want to be. We worry, we doubt, we hesitate—because we feel like we need to be flawless before we take action.

But here's the truth: embrace the mess. Embrace the mistakes, the missteps, the awkward moments, and the imperfections. Embrace the growth that comes from failing, learning, and trying again. This is where the real transformation happens. Life isn't about fitting into a perfect mold—it's about figuring out who you are, what works for you, and what makes you feel alive. It's about pushing past your insecurities and your need for validation, and instead focusing on living authentically. When you embrace the journey, the little hiccups, and the bumps along the way, you create a life that's truly yours. You stop waiting for perfection and start living for yourself.

And most importantly, embrace YOU. All of you—the messy, beautiful, perfectly imperfect version of yourself. The unique blend of qualities that make you, you. Because in the end, it's not about being perfect. It's about being real. And real is so much more powerful than perfect. The real you is the one who connects with others, who makes an impact, who laughs, learns, and lives without fear of judgment. It's the real you who grows stronger with each challenge, each failure, and each moment of self-acceptance. Perfection may seem appealing, but it's the journey of becoming the best version of yourself, flaws and all, that holds the true magic.

So, don't let perfection steal your joy. Don't let it keep you from stepping out of your comfort zone, from taking risks, and from being the bold, authentic person you were always meant to be. Let go of the pressure to be flawless, and start embracing who you truly are. Because the world doesn't need perfect. It needs real. And real is enough.

CHAPTER XI

# Why to Worry When Ambition is Not Greed

Ambition is often misunderstood. Some label it as greed, an insatiable desire for more, while others see it as a selfish pursuit of personal goals. But the truth is, ambition is far from greed—it's the spark that propels us forward, fuels our dreams, and gives purpose to our actions. Greed takes; ambition builds. Greed is self-serving; ambition uplifts not just the individual but often the people around them. When nurtured responsibly, ambition can lead to extraordinary growth and meaningful contributions to the world.

The key lies in understanding the difference between ambition and greed. Ambition is driven by a desire to improve oneself, achieve goals, and create something valuable. It stems from a place of passion and purpose. Greed, on the other hand, is fueled by an insatiable craving for more, often at the expense of others. Greed disregards ethics and empathy, while ambition works within a framework of integrity and vision.

Have you ever hesitated to share your ambitions for fear of being judged as greedy? It's a common dilemma. Society sometimes paints ambition, especially in certain contexts, as something negative. But holding back from chasing your dreams because of this misconception does a disservice not only to you but also to those who might benefit from your success. Think about the scientists, artists, and entrepreneurs who have changed the world. Their ambition wasn't about hoarding wealth or power—it was about creating, innovating, and making an impact.

Ambitions come in all shapes and sizes. Some aim for professional milestones like earning a university degree, becoming an industry expert, or climbing the corporate ladder to become a CEO. Others are deeply personal, like helping a community, mentoring new talent, or building a robust professional network. Then there are the ambitions that are bold and adventurous—like bungee jumping, climbing a mountain, attending a ball party with your date, or even publishing your own book. For me, the dream of publishing my book was an ambition I nurtured for years before finally making it a reality.

What I've realized is that every ambition, no matter how big or small, is a testament to the courage and determination within you. They reflect your willingness to dream, your capacity to step beyond the ordinary, and your belief that you are capable of achieving greatness. Life isn't just about sticking to a regular schedule or playing it safe; it's about embracing the extraordinary moments and daring to do something different. If life presents you with an opportunity to chase a dream, the real question should be: Why not? Grab the moment, make it count, and savor the journey. Sometimes, you don't even realize what you're missing until you take that leap of faith and feel the exhilaration of living your dream.

Of course, there will be people who may label you as selfish or greedy for pursuing your ambitions, especially when they don't align with their expectations. But here's the truth: your happiness isn't something that can be borrowed or dictated by others. You are the sole reason for your smile and your joy. Your ambitions, no matter how "crazy" they seem to others, are valid because they bring you closer to who you are meant to be. So stop apologizing for dreaming big or wanting something different in your life. Instead, embrace those ambitions wholeheartedly and go after them with everything you've got.

Life isn't about settling for what's comfortable—it's about pushing boundaries, discovering what truly makes you happy, and living with no regrets. Your ambitions are a roadmap to a life filled with purpose and excitement, so let them guide you. Whatever your dreams may be, know that they are yours to chase, celebrate, and achieve.

Yet, it's essential to keep ambition in check. While ambition drives us toward our goals, an unchecked desire for success can sometimes tip into greed. The line between ambition and greed often blurs when our focus shifts solely to personal gain, neglecting the impact our actions might have on others. Ambition, when driven by a desire to grow and contribute, is inspiring. However, when it becomes fueled by an insatiable need for more—more recognition, more wealth, more power—it can lose its positive essence and transform into greediness.

To avoid this pitfall, it's important to ground ambition in core values and self-awareness. Reflect on why you are pursuing your goals. Is it to grow, to challenge yourself, or to create a positive impact? Or is it simply to outdo others or accumulate possessions? Asking yourself questions like "Why do I want this?" or "What will this mean for others in my life?" can help you recalibrate your motivations. Ambition aligned with purpose and empathy not only keeps you on track but also ensures that your success benefits more than just yourself.

Another crucial step is to balance your aspirations with gratitude for what you already have. Greed often stems from a sense of lack—a belief that no matter how much you achieve, it will never be enough. By practicing gratitude, you remind yourself of the abundance already present in your life. This doesn't mean settling for less or giving up on your goals; it means appreciating the journey and finding fulfillment in progress, not just outcomes.

Lastly, consider the legacy you want to leave behind. When ambition is tied to a larger purpose—be it supporting your family, creating opportunities for others, or leaving a positive mark on your community—it transcends selfish desires. It becomes a force for good, one that inspires others and brings meaning to your achievements. True ambition isn't about stepping on others to climb higher; it's about lifting others up as you rise.

Ambition should propel you forward, but it should never blind you to what truly matters. When you pursue your dreams with integrity and empathy, ambition becomes a powerful tool to not only achieve success but also create a life of purpose and fulfillment—one that enriches not just your own, but the lives of those around you.

It's also important to remember that ambition doesn't have to be grandiose. Not everyone's ambition involves building empires, achieving fame, or revolutionizing industries. Ambition is deeply personal and can take countless forms. For some, it's about building a happy and loving family—a goal that requires dedication, emotional strength, and patience. For others, it's about contributing meaningfully to their community, whether through volunteering, mentorship, or simply being a reliable and compassionate friend. Ambition can also be as simple and profound as mastering a personal skill—learning to play a musical instrument, writing a novel, or perfecting a culinary recipe.

The scale of your ambition is irrelevant; what truly matters is its alignment with your values and the sense of fulfillment it brings. Society often glamorizes high-profile ambitions, but the quieter, more personal ones are just as important and impactful. These ambitions shape our daily lives, our relationships, and our inner sense of purpose. They remind us that success is not a one-size-fits-all concept.

Moreover, ambition doesn't have to be about constant striving or endless achievements. Sometimes, it's about finding joy in the process and celebrating small victories along the way. It's about setting goals that resonate with who you are and pursuing them with authenticity. Whether your ambition is to climb a mountain or simply to enjoy a peaceful, meaningful life, its true value lies in how it enriches your journey and helps you grow.

Ultimately, ambition should be a reflection of your unique identity and aspirations. It doesn't need to impress others or conform to societal expectations. What matters is that it fuels your passion, aligns with your principles, and allows you to create a life that feels purposeful and fulfilling. Embrace your ambitions, whatever they may be, and let them guide you toward a life that truly feels like your own.

Ambition is a powerful force, but like anything, it needs balance. How ambitious should you be? The answer lies in understanding yourself, your goals, and the life you want to create. Ambition should inspire and challenge you, but it should never consume or define you entirely.

Being ambitious doesn't mean you have to aim for unrealistic, towering goals at all times. It means setting objectives that excite and push you while remaining achievable and aligned with your values. Ambition should fuel your passion, not overwhelm your peace. Striking a balance between striving for growth and appreciating your current state is key. Life isn't just about chasing the next milestone; it's also about enjoying the moments along the way.

Another factor to consider is the impact of your ambition. How does it affect your well-being and relationships? Healthy ambition drives you to achieve without compromising your mental health or personal connections. When ambition becomes all-consuming, it can lead to burnout, stress, and strained relationships. Ask yourself: Are my goals enriching my life or draining me? If you feel more exhausted than energized, it might be time to recalibrate.

Ambition also needs to be grounded in reality. Dream big, but don't set yourself up for constant disappointment by chasing goals that are entirely unattainable in the short term. Break your larger aspirations into smaller, actionable steps. Celebrate these mini-accomplishments—they're just as important as the end goal.

Ambition should come with self-compassion. You might not achieve everything exactly as planned, and that's okay. Failure and setbacks are part of growth, not reasons to give up. Being ambitious doesn't mean you can't be kind to yourself along the way.

Ultimately, how ambitious you should be is a personal choice. It depends on what drives you, what fulfills you, and what kind of life you envision for yourself. The key is finding that sweet spot where your ambition motivates you without overwhelming you, pushing you forward while still allowing you to appreciate the journey. After all, ambition is most powerful when it's not just about achieving but about becoming the best version of yourself.

So, don't let the fear of being labeled greedy hold you back. Your ambitions are yours to define, nurture, and pursue. When guided by purpose, ambition is not a flaw—it's a gift. It's the driving force that allows you to realize your potential and leave a positive mark on the world.

As you embrace your ambitions, remember to balance them with gratitude and mindfulness. Celebrate your achievements, but don't lose sight of the journey or the people who supported you along the way. Ambition isn't about reaching the top at all costs—it's about growing into the best version of yourself while contributing meaningfully to the lives of others. So, chase your dreams unapologetically and let your ambition be the compass that guides you, knowing that it's not greed—it's the essence of progress.

CHAPTER XII

# Why to Worry When True Satisfaction is Within You

In the relentless pursuit of happiness, we often look outward—chasing material possessions, accolades, or the approval of others. We tell ourselves that once we achieve a specific milestone, acquire something new, or gain validation, we'll finally feel satisfied. However, true satisfaction isn't something that can be granted by external factors. It's an internal state of being, a deep sense of contentment that comes from understanding and appreciating who you are and what you have.

True satisfaction begins with self-awareness. It's about recognizing your values, passions, and purpose. When you align your actions with what truly matters to you, a profound sense of fulfillment follows. Have you ever noticed how some people remain content even in modest circumstances, while others with seemingly everything still feel empty? The difference lies in perspective. When you focus on your inner self rather than external measures of success, you begin to discover that satisfaction isn't something to be chased—it's something to be nurtured within.

Think about the small moments in life that bring you joy: the warmth of the sun on your face, a heartfelt conversation with a loved one, or the satisfaction of completing a task that matters to you. These moments may seem trivial, but they're rich with meaning if you allow yourself to appreciate them fully. When you learn to find joy in the simple and the present, you unlock the key to lasting satisfaction.

One of the Biggest Barriers to Inner Satisfaction: Comparison

Comparison is a thief of joy, quietly creeping into our thoughts and robbing us of contentment. In today's hyper-connected world, where everyone's highlight reel is on display, it's easy to fall into the trap of comparing our lives to others. We see friends landing dream jobs, embarking on extravagant vacations, or celebrating milestones, and we wonder, "Why isn't my life like theirs?" This constant comparison creates a sense of inadequacy, making us blind to the blessings and achievements in our own lives.

What we often fail to realize is that these comparisons are built on incomplete information. Social media and surface-level interactions rarely reveal the whole story. Everyone has their share of struggles, challenges, and insecurities, even if they're not apparent to the outside world. What appears perfect and seamless on the surface may mask significant effort, sacrifice, or difficulty. By focusing too much on others, we lose sight of our own unique journey, missing out on opportunities for personal growth and fulfillment.

To overcome the habit of comparison, it's essential to shift our mindset. Instead of measuring ourselves against others, we should learn to celebrate their successes while appreciating our own. Ask yourself: "Am I genuinely striving for my personal goals, or am I chasing something simply because it looks good in someone else's life?" When you let go of external benchmarks and tune into your own path, you'll start to find satisfaction in the progress you've made.

One of the most effective antidotes to comparison is gratitude. Gratitude is more than just saying "thank you" for the big things in life; it's a mindset that encourages you to recognize and appreciate even the smallest moments of joy. A warm cup of coffee on a chilly morning, the laughter of a friend, or even a beautiful sunset—these small blessings often go unnoticed in our quest for "more."Practicing gratitude helps shift your focus from what you lack to what you already have. It's a conscious choice to acknowledge the goodness in your life, no matter how modest it may seem. Studies have shown that people who regularly practice gratitude tend to feel happier, more optimistic, and more satisfied with their lives. Gratitude isn't just a feel-good exercise; it rewires your brain to focus on the positive, cultivating a mindset of abundance rather than scarcity.To incorporate gratitude into your daily routine, start small. At the end of each day, take a few moments to jot down three things you're thankful for. They don't have to be grand gestures or significant events. It could be as simple as a kind word from a stranger, a productive day at work, or the comfort of your favorite book. Over time, this practice helps you develop a habit of looking for the good in every situation, no matter how challenging it might seem.

When you embrace gratitude, you begin to see your life from a new perspective. Rather than envying someone else's journey, you recognize the value of your own. Every experience, whether joyous or difficult, shapes you in unique ways. Your challenges teach you resilience, your accomplishments boost your confidence, and even your missteps provide valuable lessons. Gratitude allows you to honor your journey for what it is—a work in progress, filled with its own victories and treasures.

It's also important to remember that life isn't a competition. The success of others doesn't diminish your potential or worth. There's enough room in the world for everyone to thrive in their way. When you let go of the mindset that someone else's win is your loss, you create space for collaboration, encouragement, and genuine connection.

Inner satisfaction doesn't come from keeping up with others; it comes from aligning your life with your values and recognizing the abundance already present. The next time you find yourself comparing your life to someone else's, pause and take a step back. Ask yourself what truly matters to you and what you're grateful for at this moment. You'll find that contentment isn't something you have to chase—it's already within you, waiting to be uncovered.By practicing gratitude and letting go of comparison, you reclaim your joy and take ownership of your journey. True satisfaction arises not from measuring up to others but from appreciating your progress and living in alignment with your authentic self. So, celebrate your unique path and trust that it's leading you exactly where you're meant to be.

Satisfaction also stems from living a life of purpose. Purpose doesn't have to mean grand achievements; it's about doing things that resonate with your soul. Whether it's nurturing relationships, helping others, or pursuing a hobby you love, purpose adds depth to your daily life. When you live with intention, satisfaction naturally follows, because your actions are aligned with your inner values.

Life isn't without challenges, and satisfaction doesn't mean ignoring difficulties or pretending everything is perfect. It's about facing those challenges with grace and resilience, knowing that setbacks don't define you. True satisfaction lies in how you respond to life's ups and downs, maintaining a sense of balance and hope even in the face of adversity.

Fear of losing what we have is a natural part of being human. Whether it's the fear of losing our possessions, relationships, status, or even life itself, this fear often holds us back from embracing true satisfaction. We clutch tightly to what we have, afraid that any change might disrupt our sense of stability and happiness. However, this fear begins to dissipate when we shift our perspective and understand that our life story, and indeed the broader history of the world, is written by the same hand—a hand that weaves purpose, meaning, and connection into every experience.

When we view life through this lens, we realize that everything we encounter, whether gain or loss, joy or sorrow, is part of a greater narrative. Every challenge is an opportunity to grow, and every setback is a stepping stone to something more profound. Recognizing this interconnectedness helps us to let go of fear and trust in the journey. Instead of fixating on what we might lose, we learn to appreciate what we already have and open ourselves to what could be.This perspective ties closely to the idea of finding satisfaction within ourselves. Often, we look outward for validation and fulfillment, relying on external factors to define our happiness. But true contentment arises when we understand that life's ups and downs are not meant to defeat us but to shape us. Just as a story requires both conflict and resolution to be meaningful, our lives gain depth and richness through the variety of experiences we face.

For example, consider the fear of losing a job. This fear might paralyze us, making us reluctant to take risks or explore new opportunities. But if we trust that the hand guiding our story is leading us toward growth, we can see even this potential loss as a chance to discover new paths, develop resilience, and find fulfillment in unexpected places. Instead of letting fear dictate our actions, we can focus on the strengths and capabilities we possess, knowing that we are equipped to handle whatever comes next.

Embracing this mindset doesn't mean dismissing the importance of what we have or avoiding responsibility. On the contrary, it encourages us to cherish our blessings without becoming overly attached to them. By letting go of the fear of loss, we allow ourselves to live fully in the present moment. We no longer hold back out of anxiety about the future, and we begin to recognize that satisfaction isn't found in the security of what we own but in the peace of knowing that we can navigate life's uncertainties.

So, as we reflect on the things we hold dear, let us also remind ourselves that life's story is constantly unfolding, shaped by forces far greater than our control. Trust in that narrative, and you'll find that fear no longer has the power to overshadow your joy. True satisfaction lies not in clinging to what we have but in embracing the journey with open hands and an open heart, knowing that each chapter is written with purpose and meaning.

Satisfaction isn't a destination; it's a journey. It's about finding peace in where you are right now while continuing to grow and evolve. True satisfaction doesn't come from ticking boxes off a checklist; it comes from realizing that you are enough, just as you are.

So, stop worrying about chasing satisfaction from the outside world. Instead, turn inward. Reflect on what truly matters to you, practice gratitude, and embrace the present moment. Because when you do, you'll discover that true satisfaction has been within you all along.

CHAPTER XIII

# Why to Worry When Financial Freedom is Attainable

Financial freedom is often seen as an elusive dream, but it's more achievable than many people realize. It doesn't necessarily mean having millions in the bank or retiring early to live a life of luxury. True financial freedom is about having control over your finances—where your money works for you rather than the other way around. It's about making choices that align with your values and goals, without constantly worrying about debt or financial instability.

The journey to financial freedom starts with awareness and discipline. The first step is to understand where you stand financially. Create a clear picture of your income, expenses, savings, and debts. Many people avoid looking closely at their finances out of fear or guilt, but facing the reality of your situation is empowering. Once you know where your money is going, you can identify areas for improvement and start making intentional changes.

One of the keys to financial freedom is learning to live within your means. This doesn't mean depriving yourself of joy or comfort—it's about prioritizing what truly matters. Instead of spending impulsively or trying to keep up with societal pressures, focus on what adds value to your life. A simple exercise is to differentiate between needs and wants. Satisfying your needs ensures security, while carefully choosing your wants helps you align spending with long-term happiness.

Another essential aspect of financial freedom is saving and investing. Saving isn't just about putting aside money for emergencies; it's also about creating a safety net that gives you peace of mind. Start with small, consistent contributions to a savings account, and over time, explore investment opportunities that can help your money grow. The power of compound interest is remarkable—it's like planting a tree that grows bigger with time, providing shade and fruit for years to come.

A significant step toward financial freedom is learning how to make your money work for you through smart investments. Investment is not merely about growing wealth—it's about securing your future. Here's how to approach it:

1. Start Early

Time is your best friend in investment. Starting early allows your money to benefit from compound interest, where earnings from your investments are reinvested to generate additional returns. This exponential growth can significantly increase your wealth over time.

2. Diversify Your Portfolio

"Don't put all your eggs in one basket" is a fundamental rule in investing. Diversify your investments across different asset classes like stocks, bonds, mutual funds, real estate, and even retirement funds. Diversification reduces risk and ensures that even if one investment underperforms, others can balance the loss.

3. Invest in Index Funds and ETFs

For beginners, index funds and exchange-traded funds (ETFs) are excellent options. They offer a low-cost way to invest in a broad market and minimize risks compared to individual stocks. These investments are great for long-term goals like retirement.

4. Understand Risk vs. Return

Every investment carries some risk, and understanding your risk tolerance is essential. Stocks and real estate may offer higher returns but come with higher risk, whereas bonds and savings accounts are safer but yield lower returns. Choose a mix that aligns with your financial goals and comfort level.

5. Emergency Fund Comes First

Before diving into investments, ensure you have an emergency fund equivalent to at least 3–6 months of living expenses. This fund acts as a safety net, allowing you to handle unforeseen expenses without disrupting your investments.

6. Educate Yourself

Investing is not gambling—it requires knowledge and research. Read books, attend seminars, or take online courses to understand the fundamentals of investing. The more informed you are, the better decisions you'll make.

While investments grow your wealth, it's equally important to manage your day-to-day finances wisely. Living within your means, cutting unnecessary expenses, and saving diligently are the foundation of financial stability. Set aside a portion of your income for savings and investments each month, treating it as a non-negotiable expense.

While investing for retirement is crucial, remember to balance long-term goals with short-term priorities. Plan for milestones like buying a home, traveling, or pursuing further education. Creating separate funds for these goals ensures you stay prepared while continuing to grow your wealth.

Financial freedom is not solely about accumulating wealth—it's about having choices and living without constant financial stress. Shift your mindset from scarcity to abundance. Appreciate what you have and work toward your goals with confidence. Proper investments, combined with disciplined financial habits, can provide the peace of mind that comes with knowing you're on a secure path.

Achieving financial freedom requires effort, but it is within reach for anyone willing to plan and act strategically. Start small, stay consistent, and focus on the bigger picture. With proper investments, disciplined saving, and a focus on creating a secure future, you'll find yourself stepping into a life where financial worries are replaced with possibilities and peace. After all, why worry when financial freedom is attainable?

CHAPTER XIV

# Why to Worry When Success is Yours to Maintain

Success is often viewed as the ultimate destination, but the truth is, it's a continuous journey. Achieving success is just one part of the equation; the real challenge lies in maintaining it. Sustained success requires focus, adaptability, and a willingness to grow. It's not about resting on your laurels but embracing the mindset that success isn't a one-time event—it's a lifestyle.

Ever worked tirelessly to achieve something significant and felt the joy of success, not just for yourself but for those around you? The applause, the congratulations, and the pride in others' eyes can be incredibly fulfilling. Yet, deep down, a question may linger: "What's next?" Alongside the joy of success often comes an unspoken weight—the expectations of others and the pressure to maintain your accomplishments.

You might feel like you've set a benchmark, not just for yourself but for everyone watching. The idea of having to live up to these expectations can feel overwhelming. Suddenly, it's no longer just about what you want but about fulfilling what others think you should achieve. It's easy to fall into the trap of defining your worth based on external validation.

But here's the real question: Do you want to live your life meeting others' expectations, or do you want to set new challenges for yourself, driven by your own goals and passions? Success is deeply personal. It's not about being in a race to maintain an image in someone else's eyes but about finding fulfillment in your own journey.

Instead of worrying about maintaining success just to meet societal standards, shift your focus inward. Ask yourself what you truly want from this stage of your life. Success isn't about being stagnant; it's about evolving. Use this opportunity to reflect on what excites you, what challenges you, and what you want to accomplish next—not because someone else expects it, but because it aligns with your vision.

Remember, expectations from others can be motivating, but they should never control your path. The only expectations that truly matter are the ones you set for yourself. Take ownership of your journey, embrace the challenges that come with success, and view them as opportunities to grow. After all, life isn't about maintaining a static peak; it's about reaching for the next summit.

By doing this, you transform the fear of maintaining success into a driving force for new achievements. You turn external pressures into internal motivation. Success then becomes not just something to hold onto but a catalyst for future possibilities. So, instead of worrying about keeping up with the expectations of others, ask yourself: What do I want to achieve next? Once you have the answer, pursue it with the same dedication that brought you success in the first place.

Ultimately, maintaining success isn't about fulfilling others' dreams; it's about embracing your own.

Success isn't static; it evolves as you do. What worked to get you where you are might not always keep you there. Industries change, skills become outdated, and new challenges arise. Maintaining success demands the ability to anticipate change and adapt accordingly.

Take, for instance, a successful entrepreneur who has built a thriving business. If they stop innovating or ignore market trends, competitors will quickly outpace them. However, by staying informed, investing in their team, and continuously improving their offerings, they can maintain their success and stay ahead.

The key to maintaining success lies in lifelong learning. The world is dynamic, and staying stagnant is not an option. Embrace opportunities to learn new skills, expand your knowledge, and challenge yourself.Think of a professional athlete. They may have natural talent, but to stay at the top of their game, they must train rigorously, adapt to new strategies, and overcome injuries or setbacks. Similarly, success in any field requires constant effort and evolution.

Maintaining success can be as challenging as achieving it in the first place. Many individuals, after reaching significant milestones, find it difficult to sustain their accomplishments. This often raises the question: Why do some people fail to maintain success, and how can these pitfalls be avoided?

One of the primary reasons people lose success is complacency. After achieving their goals, some individuals become comfortable and stop striving for growth, assuming their momentum will carry them forward. However, success requires continuous effort and vigilance. Another common issue is the fear of change. Success often brings new challenges and responsibilities, and fear of stepping out of one's comfort zone or adapting to new circumstances can lead to stagnation. Similarly, neglecting relationships plays a significant role in the downfall of success. Many fail to recognize that achievements are rarely a solo effort; ignoring the support systems that contributed to their success can create isolation and hinder future progress. Lastly, the mindset that there's no longer a need for self-improvement can be detrimental. The world evolves constantly, and staying relevant requires a commitment to lifelong learning and growth.

To avoid losing success, it's crucial to stay humble and curious. Success should be treated as a stepping stone rather than a final destination. Continuously learning, exploring, and striving for excellence helps individuals remain motivated and grounded. Setting new goals is another important strategy. After reaching one milestone, defining new objectives—whether big or small—ensures that you keep progressing and don't fall into complacency. Embracing change is equally vital, as adaptability is often the key to long-term success. Being open to new ideas and staying informed about trends helps you stay relevant in a rapidly changing world.

Success isn't achieved—or maintained—in isolation. Surround yourself with people who inspire, challenge, and support you.

Mentors, colleagues, friends, and family can provide valuable feedback and keep you grounded. A strong support system also helps you navigate the pressures and responsibilities that come with success.Maintaining strong relationships is another critical factor. Acknowledging and appreciating the contributions of those who supported you is essential. Collaboration and a robust support system can help you navigate challenges and sustain your achievements. Self-reflection also plays an integral role in maintaining success. Regularly evaluating your progress, identifying areas for improvement, and adjusting strategies can provide valuable insights for the future. Additionally, balancing ambition with gratitude is key. While pursuing new goals, taking time to appreciate how far you've come fosters a sense of fulfillment and prevents burnout.Ultimately, maintaining success is about evolving with the present while preparing for the future.

Even after achieving success, setbacks are inevitable. The path is rarely smooth, but resilience is what sets those who sustain success apart. Instead of viewing failures as the end of the road, see them as opportunities to learn and grow. Each setback is a stepping stone to greater achievements.

Consider the inspiring story of J.K. Rowling, the globally celebrated author of the Harry Potter series. Her journey to success wasn't easy—she faced countless rejections before her first book was published. When Harry Potter and the Philosopher's Stone became a runaway success, it catapulted her into international fame and brought her immense recognition. But with that success came a new challenge: how to sustain it. Would she be a one-hit wonder, or would she continue to thrive in the literary world?

Rowling didn't allow the fear of meeting expectations or maintaining her success to paralyze her. Instead, she embraced her newfound platform and stayed true to her passion for storytelling. She completed the Harry Potter series, each installment met with growing anticipation and acclaim. But Rowling didn't stop there. Instead of resting on her laurels, she took bold steps to challenge herself creatively. She ventured into new genres, writing crime fiction under the pseudonym Robert Galbraith and publishing adult novels such as The Casual Vacancy. Through this, she demonstrated an essential truth about success: it isn't just about reaching a peak; it's about evolving and staying authentic to your passion.

Her story offers a powerful lesson for anyone worried about maintaining success. Rowling could have chosen to limit herself to the safety of the familiar, repeating the same formula that had worked for her before. Instead, she took risks, embraced change, and allowed herself to grow as a writer. By doing so, she turned her initial success into a long-lasting legacy, proving that success is not a static achievement but an ongoing journey.Her journey also highlights that maintaining success isn't about clinging to what you've already achieved but about finding ways to build upon it.

Use your achievements as a foundation for growth, not as a destination. Ask yourself what inspires you, what excites you, and what new avenues you can explore. Remember, success isn't about holding onto one moment—it's about creating a lifetime of meaningful accomplishments. Like Rowling, let your success be the beginning of a much greater story.

When you achieve success, it comes with responsibility—not just to yourself but to others who look up to you. Use your success to inspire and uplift others. Share your knowledge, mentor those who are starting their journey, and give back to the community. This not only helps others but also reinforces your own sense of purpose and fulfillment.

Grit—a simple word with a powerful meaning. By definition, it means courage and determination despite difficulty. But its true essence hit me during a session arranged by my scholarship program at a higher institute. The CEO of the company leading the session shared a perspective that left a lasting impact on me. He explained that grit is more than just perseverance; it's the perfect blend of passion and persistence. It's about pouring your heart into your goals, putting in relentless effort until you succeed. And if you fail? You double down, try again, and keep pushing forward. Grit is the refusal to settle until you achieve what you truly desire. That day, I realized grit isn't just a trait; it's a mindset that maintains success.

So, why worry when success is yours to maintain? True success isn't a fleeting moment; it's a steady rhythm you create through consistency, adaptability, and purpose. It's not about reaching a peak and fearing the descent but about building a foundation so strong that even setbacks become stepping stones. Remember, sustaining success means staying curious, embracing growth, and never settling for complacency. Celebrate your wins, but always look ahead with a mindset of abundance and resilience. After all, success isn't just something you achieve—it's something you embody, day by day, decision by decision.

CHAPTER XV

# Why to Worry When Freedom is in Your Choices

Life is a series of choices, from the seemingly insignificant—what to eat for breakfast—to the monumental—where to live, who to love, and what path to take. Each decision reflects not just our preferences but also our power. Freedom isn't just about living without restrictions; it's about realizing that you hold the reins to shape your life, one choice at a time.

Think about it: every day, you're presented with countless options, each one an opportunity to express your individuality. Yet, choices can feel overwhelming, especially when they come with risks, consequences, or the weight of societal expectations. The fear of making the "wrong" choice can paralyze us, leaving us stuck in indecision. But here's the truth: there is no such thing as a perfect decision. Every choice teaches you something—either it leads to growth or offers a valuable lesson.

However, it's crucial to recognize when your decisions are no longer your own. Too often, we let others' opinions, expectations, or subtle manipulations steer us toward choices that don't align with our true desires. Perhaps it's the well-meaning advice of a family member urging you to follow a traditional career path when your heart yearns for something unconventional. Or maybe it's peer pressure convincing you to act against your instincts just to fit in. These external influences, while sometimes helpful, can cloud your judgment and disconnect you from your own needs and aspirations.

Freedom lies in reclaiming the power to make your own choices, uninfluenced by others' agendas. It's about pausing to reflect on what you want, not what others think is best for you. Ask yourself: Am I making this decision because it aligns with my goals, or am I doing it to please someone else? The answer can be incredibly revealing. True freedom means resisting the pull of external pressures and standing firm in your beliefs and desires.

Making choices under the pressure of others often leads to regret. It may seem easier in the moment to go along with what someone else wants, but over time, you'll feel the weight of living a life that isn't authentically yours. That's why it's so important to trust yourself and your instincts. Give yourself the permission to choose based on your own happiness and priorities.

Remember, no one else can fully understand your dreams, values, or the intricacies of your life. They might mean well, but they don't walk in your shoes. By allowing their opinions to override your inner voice, you're giving away your freedom—the very thing that allows you to carve out a life of meaning and fulfillment.

Freedom is not about rebelling against advice or ignoring constructive input; it's about discerning which guidance aligns with your values and goals. Take in what resonates, but don't feel obligated to follow a path that doesn't feel right. Stand your ground, be assertive, and protect your choices.

Freedom lies in understanding that your choices are yours alone. They don't need to be justified to others or align with anyone else's idea of success or happiness. Want to quit that high-paying job to pursue your passion for painting? Do it. Want to move to a new city, even if people call it impractical? Go ahead. Freedom doesn't mean living recklessly—it means living authentically, in alignment with your values and desires.

Sometimes, though, the hardest choices are the ones that challenge our comfort zones. Choosing to walk away from toxic relationships, leaving a path that doesn't fulfill you, or standing up for yourself in difficult situations requires courage. But these moments are where freedom truly shines. It's about saying, I deserve better, and acting on it.

In a Formula One race, every lap brings new challenges. Some corners are sharp and unpredictable, requiring quick reflexes and calculated risks. Not every turn can be executed with the perfect gear change or ideal speed. Drivers know this—they don't aim for perfection in every moment; they aim to adapt, recalibrate, and move forward. This mindset mirrors the essence of freedom and choice in life.

Just like a race, life doesn't come with a flawless track. Every choice you make is like navigating a corner—some you'll take smoothly, others might shake your confidence. The beauty lies not in achieving perfection but in embracing the process. Freedom means accepting that you won't always get it right, and that's okay. What matters is that you're in the driver's seat, steering your life according to your instincts, values, and aspirations.

Mistakes, like misjudged corners in a race, are inevitable. But instead of seeing them as failures, view them as opportunities to adjust your approach. Maybe you took a decision too hastily or hesitated when boldness was required. Each choice, whether it propels you forward or slows you down momentarily, contributes to your growth. Freedom isn't about a seamless journey; it's about navigating the twists and turns with resilience and self-trust.

The key is to keep moving. In Formula One, the worst thing a driver can do is stop mid-track, paralyzed by a mistake. Similarly, in life, don't let fear of imperfect choices freeze you in indecision. Keep going, learning with every turn, and refining your strategy as you go. Freedom lies in the courage to take the next lap, knowing you have the power to course-correct and improve.

Remember, just like a race, life's ultimate goal isn't a flawless performance—it's reaching the finish line with a story of persistence, courage, and authenticity. So, embrace the laps, the corners, the missteps, and the triumphs. Each choice, even the imperfect ones, is a testament to your freedom to live a life true to yourself.

Ultimately, the freedom to choose your own path is a gift. Don't squander it by letting others dictate your decisions. Own your freedom, embrace your choices, and move forward with confidence, knowing that even if you stumble, at least you're living life on your own terms.

Freedom to make your own choices is like being handed the keys to a world full of possibilities. Think of it as walking into an ice cream parlor with endless flavors. Some choices will be a hit—double fudge brownie, anyone? Others, like pickle-flavored ice cream, might be a complete miss. But hey, at least you tried! That's the beauty of it: every decision, good or bad, adds a little more flavor to your life story.

Don't stress over making the "perfect" choice, because perfection is overrated. Life is about experiences, not flawless execution. Imagine you're at a crossroads, and one path looks easy and predictable, while the other seems like an adventure waiting to unfold. Why not choose the adventurous one once in a while? After all, the memories you create are often from the unexpected detours, not the perfectly planned routes.

And here's the thing about freedom: it's not just about the big life decisions like careers and relationships. It's also in the small, everyday moments. Dancing in the kitchen while making dinner, trying a new hobby you've always been curious about, or even choosing to take a mental health day when you need it. These little acts of freedom remind you that life is yours to shape.

So, when faced with choices, approach them with curiosity, not fear. Ask yourself, "What's the worst that could happen?" Often, the worst isn't nearly as scary as your mind makes it out to be. Give yourself the gift of experimenting with life, laughing at the missteps, and celebrating the victories—because freedom to choose isn't a burden. It's the ultimate privilege to create a life that feels uniquely and authentically yours.

From the time we were children, freedom was the ultimate dream. We craved it in every little thing—choosing what to wear, deciding which cartoon to watch, staying up late, or heading out for adventures with friends. Every time we heard "No" or "You're too young for that," it only fueled our longing to grow up and claim the freedom we thought would make life perfect. Attending birthday parties, having sleepovers, and planning nights out seemed like the ultimate luxuries that adulthood promised. Yet, in those moments, our parents held the reins, ensuring our safety, guiding us, and making decisions they believed were best for us.

Back then, their rules and restrictions often felt like barriers. "Why can't I go?" or "Why don't they trust me?" were common frustrations. But looking back, wasn't it comforting to know someone else was shouldering the responsibility? They were our safety net, sparing us from the weight of making big decisions. Childhood, in hindsight, wasn't just about yearning for freedom; it was about feeling secure in the knowledge that someone else had our back. Someone who would catch us if we fell.

But then comes adulthood—the stage we eagerly awaited. Suddenly, the freedom we wanted so badly is right in front of us, but it comes with a catch: responsibility. There's no one to ask permission from now, no one to guide us through the maze of decisions. It's entirely up to us. Do we take that job offer? Move to a new city? Trust someone with our feelings? The choices that once felt liberating now carry the weight of potential consequences.

As adults, we often catch ourselves reminiscing about the simplicity of childhood—the days when someone else navigated the stormy seas while we played on the deck. Now, we're the captains of our own ships, and the vast ocean of possibilities can feel overwhelming. It's not unusual to think, "Maybe it was better when I didn't have to decide everything myself."

But here's the truth: this transition is a rite of passage. Growing up means learning to embrace the freedom that age grants us, even when it feels daunting. It's about understanding that while choices may be difficult, they're also empowering. We're no longer just living under someone else's guidance; we're creating our own path. Yes, there will be missteps—times when we wish someone had told us what to do. But there will also be triumphs—moments when we make a choice, and it turns out to be exactly what we needed.

So, as you face the reality of freedom, remember this: you're not alone in feeling the weight of responsibility. Everyone transitions from longing for independence to realizing it's a double-edged sword. Use this freedom to honor the lessons you learned as a child. Make choices that reflect your growth, your values, and your dreams. Because while freedom might feel heavy at times, it's also the most beautiful gift of growing up—a chance to live authentically and on your own terms.

CHAPTER XVI

# Why to Worry When You Belong in Any League

We've all been there—standing in a room full of people who seem smarter, more accomplished, or just inherently "better" in some intangible way. Maybe it's a new workplace, a social gathering, or even a gym where everyone seems to know what they're doing except you. The feeling is universal, and it has a name: imposter syndrome. It creeps in with whispers like, "You don't belong here," "You're not good enough," or "What if they find out you're a fraud?" But here's the thing: you do belong. You've earned your place in every league you find yourself in.

Think about it—every expert was once a beginner. Every accomplished professional has doubted themselves at some point. No one is born knowing all the answers or brimming with confidence. Belonging isn't about being perfect; it's about showing up, being present, and contributing in your unique way. The moment you step into that room, that job, or that opportunity, you've already proven you belong. The real question isn't whether you're good enough; it's whether you believe it.

Let's address the elephant in the room: the idea that there are "leagues" at all. Society loves to categorize people—this league is for the intellectuals, that one is for the creatives, and over there is the league of social butterflies. But here's the reality: leagues are arbitrary. They're constructs built on comparison, and they crumble the moment you realize you're not competing with anyone but yourself. Your worth isn't determined by some invisible hierarchy. You belong wherever you choose to be, simply because you bring something irreplaceable: you.

Conquering the "Not Good Enough" Narrative. It's easy to spiral into self-doubt when you focus on what you lack. Maybe you don't have the years of experience someone else does, or your social skills don't shine as brightly in a crowd. But here's a little truth: you're probably overlooking the abundance of strengths and uniqueness you already have. Picture this: you're at a dessert buffet, and your plate is piled high with an assortment of treats—rich chocolate cake, delicate macarons, creamy cheesecake. But instead of savoring the spread, you're sulking about the fact that they're out of tiramisu. It sounds ridiculous, right? Yet this is exactly what we do when we fixate on what we're missing rather than appreciating what we bring to the table.

The same idea applies to life. Sure, you might not have the perfect public speaking skills or the connections of someone else in the room, but what about the creativity that helps you find solutions others might miss? What about your ability to empathize, making people feel seen and understood? Or your unique perspective, shaped by experiences no one else has lived? These are the desserts already on your plate, and they deserve to be celebrated.

Let's take an example: imagine a team brainstorming session at work. You're sitting there, nervous because you're not the loudest or most assertive voice in the room. While others toss out big, bold ideas, you hesitate, worried your suggestions won't measure up. But when you finally share your thoughts, they're met with appreciation because they bring a fresh perspective—one that balances creativity with practicality. That's your strength, and it's something no one else could have contributed in the same way.

The truth is, everyone's plate looks different. Some might have a little more tiramisu, while others have an extra helping of brownies. But the variety is what makes life, and every group you're a part of, richer. Instead of worrying about what you lack, focus on enjoying and maximizing what you already have. Your voice, your ideas, your story—they're valuable because they're yours, and no one else can replicate them.

So the next time you feel like you don't measure up, take a moment and change the perspective. Ask yourself, "What do I bring to the table?" Then, celebrate those things unapologetically.

Remember, life isn't about having a perfect plate—it's about appreciating the delicious spread you already have and savoring every bit of it.

Confidence Isn't Born—It's Built. Confidence isn't some magical trait you're born with—it's a skill you cultivate, step by step, through experience and effort. Think of it like building a muscle at the gym. The first time you lift weights, it feels awkward and difficult, and you may not see results right away. But with consistency and determination, you get stronger. Confidence works the same way—it's the result of repeatedly stepping out of your comfort zone and proving to yourself that you're capable.

One of the most common misconceptions about confidence is that it's reserved for the naturally charismatic or talented. In reality, confidence grows when you try, fail, and try again. It's in the moments when you show up despite feeling unsure, when you take that leap of faith, or when you stand up for yourself even if your voice shakes. Each of these small wins builds a reservoir of self-trust that becomes the foundation of your confidence.

Start by setting small, achievable goals. Maybe it's speaking up in a meeting, introducing yourself to someone new, or tackling a task you've been avoiding. Each time you accomplish one of these goals, you're sending a message to your brain: "I can do this." Over time, these small victories snowball, creating a sense of self-assurance that no one can take away.

It's also important to remember that confidence isn't about being perfect or knowing all the answers—it's about trusting your ability to figure things out as you go. Picture someone walking into a room with their head held high and a genuine smile. They might not have all the skills or knowledge yet, but they're willing to learn and adapt. That's true confidence: believing in your capacity to grow, no matter the situation.

Even setbacks can be confidence boosters in disguise. Every time you stumble and get back up, you're reinforcing your resilience. You're proving to yourself that you can handle challenges and that failure isn't the end of the road—it's just part of the journey.

Finally, don't underestimate the power of self-talk. The way you speak to yourself matters. Replace the "I can't" with "I'll try" and the "I'm not good enough" with "I'm learning and improving." Confidence isn't about being flawless; it's about being kind to yourself and recognizing that you're capable of growth.

So, if you've ever envied someone else's confidence, remember this: they built it, just like you can. All it takes is the willingness to start, the courage to keep going, and the determination to believe in yourself even on the hard days. Confidence is within your reach, one step at a time.

Sometimes, the fear of not belonging comes from a fear of judgment or criticism. But no one's opinion can diminish your worth unless you let it. Feedback is valuable, but it's not the ultimate truth. Take what's constructive, leave what's unnecessary, and remember that everyone—yes, even your harshest critic—has faced insecurities of their own. Criticism doesn't define you; your response to it does.

Belonging isn't about reaching a finish line where you suddenly feel secure and validated. It's about embracing the journey of growth and learning. The next time you find yourself questioning your place, remind yourself that belonging isn't a destination—it's a mindset. You belong because you're willing to show up, try, and grow.

CHAPTER XVII

# Why to Worry When Judgment Can't Define You

We've all felt the sting of judgment. A critical comment, a disapproving glance, or even a passing remark can echo in our minds far longer than it should. It's human nature to seek approval, but when we let others' opinions shape how we see ourselves, we hand over the reins of our self-worth. But here's the truth: no one's judgment can truly define you.

Judgment is often a reflection of the person making it rather than the one receiving it. People project their insecurities, biases, and fears onto others, and their opinions are filtered through their experiences. What someone thinks of you is not a universal truth—it's a perception, and perceptions are inherently flawed. So why let something so subjective dictate your self-image?

Imagine walking into a room full of mirrors, each distorting your reflection differently. Some mirrors might make you look taller, others shorter, some might warp your face altogether. Would you let those distorted reflections convince you that you're not who you are? That's precisely what judgment is—a distorted mirror. The real you remains constant, no matter how others choose to see you.

Judging a person only defines them if they allow the judgment to define them. This profound truth highlights the importance of perspective in dealing with external criticism. Judgment often reflects more about the one passing it than the one receiving it. People project their insecurities, biases, and assumptions through judgment, often without full understanding or context. When you internalize their words, you allow their limited perspective to shape your narrative, giving away control over your self-definition.

The key to resisting this lies in understanding where your self-worth truly comes from. It's not determined by fleeting opinions or external validation but by your own values, efforts, and accomplishments. Building a strong sense of self-awareness helps you recognize what defines you and creates an inner compass that is less swayed by others' judgments. When you're grounded in your identity, those judgments become background noise rather than defining statements.

A crucial part of this process is learning not to personalize judgments. People's opinions about you are often shaped by their own experiences, not yours. They might criticize your career choice, lifestyle, or even your personality, but their judgment doesn't change the reality of who you are. A strong sense of self-acceptance allows you to separate the truth of your identity from the assumptions others impose upon you.

Reframing judgment is another way to deflect its impact. Instead of seeing it as an attack, consider it an opportunity to reflect and grow. While not all judgments are valid, some can offer valuable insights or perspectives you might have overlooked. Accepting constructive feedback and discarding baseless criticism ensures that judgment serves you rather than hinders you.

The quote, "Every time you judge, you reveal an unhealed part of yourself," is often attributed to Dr. Wayne Dyer, a renowned self-help author and motivational speaker. This insight offers profound wisdom into the nature of judgment and its origins.

At its core, the quote suggests that judgment is often a reflection of our inner world rather than an accurate assessment of others. When we judge someone harshly, it typically stems from unresolved insecurities, fears, or past experiences that we project outward. For example, criticizing someone's ambition might reveal our own feelings of inadequacy or fear of failure. This perspective encourages self-reflection whenever we feel compelled to judge others, helping us uncover and address the unhealed wounds within ourselves.

The fear of judgment can be paralyzing. It might hold you back from taking risks, expressing yourself, or pursuing your dreams. You might think, "What will people say if I fail?" But consider this:

even if you succeed, someone, somewhere, will still have something negative to say. It's impossible to please everyone, so why try? Instead, focus on pleasing the one person who matters most—you.

Dealing with judgment requires resilience and self-awareness. Start by asking yourself: Do I believe this judgment is valid? Does it align with what I know to be true about myself? If the answer is no, let it go. You don't have to carry every opinion that comes your way. Learn to differentiate between constructive criticism, which helps you grow, and baseless judgment, which only aims to tear you down.

Shutting down a judgmental person doesn't mean engaging in conflict or proving them wrong. Instead, it's about maintaining your dignity, setting boundaries, and protecting your peace of mind. When faced with judgment, remember that it often reflects more about the other person's insecurities or biases than it does about you. Refusing to take their comments personally disarms their attempts to diminish your confidence. Setting boundaries is also crucial; you can politely but firmly let them know their comments are unwelcome, saying something like, "I appreciate your perspective, but I'd rather not discuss this." Responding with kindness instead of defensiveness can further diffuse negativity—thanking them for their opinion and redirecting the conversation often works wonders.

Sometimes, however, it's necessary to calmly call out their behavior using "I" statements, such as, "I feel uncomfortable when you say things like that." If the judgments persist or cross a line, consider limiting your interactions with such individuals. Surround yourself with people who uplift and support you, as a positive environment helps you stay confident and unaffected by negativity. Ultimately, the strongest defense against judgment is self-assurance. When you embrace your strengths and stay true to your values, others' opinions lose their power. By gracefully handling judgmental people, you reclaim control over your narrative and prove that no one's criticism can define your worth.

"Stop silently judging people." It's a phrase that carries both a challenge and an invitation. Judging others—especially silently—can feel harmless, almost instinctive, but its ripple effects can be profound, not just for the person being judged but also for you. Let's unpack this.

When you silently judge someone, you're not saying the words out loud, but the thoughts are there: Why are they dressed like that? Why do they talk so much? Why aren't they more ambitious? These judgments don't stay isolated in your mind; they subtly influence how you perceive and interact with that person. You might unknowingly treat them differently, or miss out on understanding their story because your thoughts have already built an invisible wall.

Here's the thing: judgment often says more about the person doing the judging than the one being judged. It's like a mirror reflecting insecurities, biases, or unmet expectations. Ask yourself: Why am I thinking this way? What does this judgment say about me? More often than not, you'll realize it stems from comparison, fear, or even a lack of self-acceptance.

Stopping silent judgment doesn't mean ignoring behaviors or opinions you don't agree with; it means replacing criticism with curiosity. Instead of thinking, Why are they like this? ask, What might their story be? This mindset shift doesn't just create empathy—it frees you from the negativity that judgment breeds. Carrying judgment is like holding onto a bag of rocks; the more you judge, the heavier it gets. Letting go lightens your mental and emotional load.

Imagine a world where, instead of silently critiquing someone's choices, you focus on your own growth and happiness. You'll find that life becomes less about measuring others and more about becoming the best version of yourself.

To address judgment effectively, you can adopt a strategy I like to call "Flip the Switch." This approach is all about transforming how you perceive and respond to judgment—whether it comes from others or from within. Instead of letting judgment weigh you down or define you, flip the narrative. Shift your focus from what others think to what truly matters: your own values, growth, and happiness.

Imagine judgment as a dimmer switch—when the criticism starts to darken your mindset, you take control and flip it toward positivity and empowerment. For example, if someone criticizes your choices, instead of internalizing their words, use the moment as an opportunity to affirm your convictions. Ask yourself: Is this judgment constructive or just noise? More often than not, you'll find it's noise—and that's your cue to switch off its impact on your emotions.

Flipping the switch can also mean using judgment as fuel for self-improvement. When faced with criticism that has merit, acknowledge it, learn from it, and move forward stronger. For instance, if someone comments on an area where you can improve, embrace it as a chance to grow rather than as an attack on your worth.

This strategy is about regaining control. Judgment, left unchecked, can feel like an external force controlling your narrative. But when you flip the switch, you reclaim your power. You remind yourself that while you can't control what others think or say, you can control how you respond. This mental shift not only frees you from the chains of judgment but also fosters a deeper sense of self-worth and resilience. So the next time judgment tries to dim your light, remember—you hold the switch. Flip it, and shine unapologetically.

Ever had one of those moments when you're so thrilled about something—like you've just nailed a presentation, finally learned that TikTok dance, or even baked a cake that didn't collapse—and then bam, someone swoops in with their unsolicited judgment? "Oh, you're proud of that? I mean, I guess it's okay, but I would've done it this way..." And just like that, your high-flying happiness takes a nosedive. You feel your excitement shrink, frustration bubble up, and suddenly you're asking yourself: Why do I even bother?

Well, my friend, this is the perfect time to Flip the Switch. Imagine their judgment is like static noise on a radio—annoying, yes, but completely within your control to turn off. Instead of letting their comments dampen your mood, consciously shift your focus back to your joy. Remind yourself: This happiness is mine, and I'm not giving it up that easily. Think of it as reclaiming your emotional turf.

Here's a trick—mentally label their comments for what they are: just opinions, not facts. Smile, nod, or if you're feeling extra spicy, say something like, "Thanks for your perspective!" (Because let's be honest, it's not like you asked for it.) Then, internally flip that mental switch: This moment is about me, not them. Revisit why you were happy in the first place and bask in your own glow.

For added humor, picture their judgment as a deflated balloon that you just toss into the wind. Or better yet, imagine them sitting at a judge's table with imaginary scorecards, while you confidently perform your life's "routine" knowing you're crushing it no matter what score they give. Why? Because your happiness isn't up for debate—it's yours to enjoy.

Flipping the switch here isn't about ignoring people completely; it's about protecting your vibe. Let them have their opinions, sure—but don't let those opinions live rent-free in your head. Keep your happiness high, let the judgments roll off, and maybe even treat yourself to another slice of that cake you baked so fabulously. Because why not?

The most empowering realization is this: the only opinion that truly defines you is your own. When you live authentically and align your actions with your values, you become immune to the noise of judgment. People will always have something to say, but their words lose power when you stand firmly in your truth.

So, the next time you feel the weight of someone's judgment, remind yourself: you are not their perception. You are not their critique. You are not their fleeting opinion. You are you, and that's enough.

Finally, remember that your life is your story to write. No one else holds the pen unless you let them. Reclaiming control of your narrative means choosing not to let judgment dictate your path. Instead, use it as fuel to live authentically and prove to yourself—not others—what you're truly capable of achieving.

CHAPTER XVIII

# Why to Worry When Disappointment is Just a Detour

We've all experienced it—the sinking feeling in your chest when things don't go as planned. Whether it's a project that didn't turn out as expected, a goal that remains just out of reach, or an opportunity you thought was yours slipping through your fingers, disappointment can feel like the end of the road. But here's the truth: disappointment is never the end. It's simply a detour on your journey, a moment that asks you to take a different route toward the same destination.

When you experience disappointment, it's easy to feel like you've hit a brick wall. But let's reframe it: what if that wall wasn't meant to stop you, but rather to push you in a different direction? Growth is rarely comfortable, and disappointment has a unique way of making you confront things you might otherwise avoid. It forces you to step out of your comfort zone, reevaluate your choices, and explore alternatives you hadn't considered.

In moments of disappointment, it's easy to fall into the trap of thinking that all your hard work was for nothing, that you're not good enough, or that you'll never get another chance. But that mindset only keeps you stuck. It's in those times, when life doesn't go according to plan, that the greatest lessons are often hidden. Disappointment is like a wake-up call—it shakes us, makes us reflect, and nudges us in a direction that we might not have considered before. If you think about it, the most successful people didn't achieve their dreams on the first try. They faced setbacks, failures, and disappointments. But instead of letting those moments define them, they used them as stepping stones.

Disappointment is not a reflection of your worth. It doesn't mean you're failing; it means you're on the verge of growth.

Consider a time when you've felt disappointed in the past. Maybe it was a job you didn't get, a relationship that ended, or a goal you didn't meet. At that moment, it may have felt like your world was crashing down. But, looking back, you can probably see how that disappointment led you to something even better—a new opportunity, a new path, a new perspective. That's because disappointment often carries with it the seed of something greater.

When life throws you a curveball, it's tempting to want to give up. But rather than focusing on the setback, ask yourself, "What can I learn from this?" Disappointment invites reflection. It challenges us to reassess our goals, our approach, and sometimes, even our entire mindset. This is where growth happens—not in the moments of success, but in the moments of discomfort, frustration, and, yes, disappointment. It's in those moments that you learn to adapt, adjust, and come back stronger.

Take Thomas Edison, for example. When he was inventing the light bulb, he faced hundreds of failures. But he didn't let those disappointments stop him. Instead, he saw each failure as a lesson in what didn't work, which ultimately led him to the breakthrough that changed the world. Edison's famous quote, "I have not failed. I've just found 10,000 ways that won't work," perfectly encapsulates the mindset you need to adopt when facing disappointment. Instead of seeing it as a roadblock, embrace it as a part of the process.

A Mirror, Not a Verdict.Disappointment doesn't always stem from a lack of effort. Sometimes, you know deep in your heart that you gave your absolute best—you put in the time, the energy, the sleepless nights—and yet, the outcome didn't align with your expectations. It's natural to feel frustrated in such moments. After all, if you're putting in the work, isn't it fair to expect a good outcome?

Yes, it is. But here's an important truth: life doesn't always unfold according to a simple equation of effort in and results out. There's an element of unpredictability, a mix of factors beyond your control—circumstances, timing, and yes, even luck. Does this mean your efforts were in vain? Absolutely not. What life offers you at each turn is a culmination of your deeds, your persistence, and, sometimes, a dash of luck you were born with.

The key here is perspective. If you know in your heart that you did everything in your power, let that knowledge be your anchor. No one else can truly understand the effort you've put in, the sacrifices you've made, or the battles you've fought within yourself to push forward. So don't let the world's judgment or a single disappointing outcome define you. And certainly, don't let disappointment seep into your mind, setting up camp and clouding your vision. You've got too much to achieve, too much potential to explore, to let one setback derail your progress.

Now, let's talk about another kind of disappointment—the one that stems from misplaced expectations. Sometimes, we hope for results without putting in the necessary effort. It's like planting a seed but forgetting to water it, then feeling let down when it doesn't bloom. This isn't disappointment—it's a reality check. You must earn the right to expect results. If you haven't truly given your best, take a step back, reassess, and start again with renewed focus. Disappointment in such cases isn't unfair; it's life's way of reminding you that there's more work to be done.

Facing the Reality Check.When disappointment stems from misplaced expectations, it often feels like a harsh wake-up call. But in reality, it's the clarity you need to grow. Facing the truth isn't about admitting failure—it's about recalibrating your approach and aligning your actions with your ambitions. These moments of realization may be uncomfortable, but they also bring invaluable insights. They force you to pause and reflect, asking yourself tough yet necessary questions: Did I truly give my best effort? Was my preparation consistent? Were my expectations realistic?If you find gaps in your answers, don't view them as failures. Instead, take them as opportunities for improvement. Disappointment in this context isn't punishment; it's life nudging you to adjust your perspective. A reality check, while it may sting at first, can ignite the determination to try harder, to strategize smarter, or to approach your goal differently.

Turning Awareness into Action.Once you recognize where the misalignment lies—whether in your efforts, your strategy, or the feasibility of your expectations—it's time to move from self-reflection to action. Begin by taking ownership of the outcome. Owning your part in the process doesn't mean blaming yourself; it means acknowledging where you could have done better and committing to change. This act of accountability empowers you to take control and reshape your path forward.As you rebuild, focus on setting clear, achievable goals. Break down your aspirations into smaller, more manageable steps. Each milestone you achieve will not only bring you closer to your ultimate objective but will also restore your confidence in your abilities. Along the way, take time to learn from the experience. Reflect on what didn't work and why. Did you overlook certain details? Were there areas where you weren't consistent? Treat every setback as a lesson and adjust your approach accordingly.

Honesty with yourself is essential during this process. If you know deep down that you didn't give your best effort, admit it to yourself without judgment. Use that truth as a catalyst for renewed commitment. The next time you approach your goal, ensure that your actions align with the results you hope to achieve. And don't be afraid to seek guidance when needed. Sometimes, an outside perspective—a mentor, a teacher, or a friend—can provide clarity that you might miss on your own.

Building Resilience Through Reality Checks.The true power of a reality check lies in its ability to build resilience. Each time you confront your shortcomings and take action, you strengthen your capacity to bounce back. Resilience doesn't mean you won't feel disappointed; it means you'll know how to respond when you do. Instead of dwelling on the setback, you'll see it as an opportunity to grow stronger, wiser, and more focused.Reality checks teach you to accept imperfection without losing hope and to keep pushing forward despite the obstacles in your way. They remind you that setbacks are not the end of the story but a part of the process. Each time you face the truth and adapt, you're not only overcoming disappointment—you're preparing yourself for greater challenges and successes ahead.

As uncomfortable as they may feel in the moment, reality checks are gifts. They strip away illusions and force you to focus on what truly matters: your effort, your mindset, and your willingness to persevere. They remind you that success is not handed out freely—it's earned through determination, persistence, and a relentless commitment to growth.These moments of clarity also serve as grounding experiences, preventing you from becoming lost in unrealistic fantasies. They redirect you toward meaningful, achievable goals that align with your values and aspirations. Reality checks aren't barriers; they're guideposts, pointing you toward a better path.

Disappointment and reality checks are not detours away from success—they're an integral part of the journey. They test your character, strengthen your resolve, and teach you invaluable lessons about persistence and adaptability. When life presents you with a reality check, don't shy away from it. Embrace it. Use it as a tool to refine your approach and reignite your determination.

In those moments, remember that it's not the setback that defines you—it's your response to it. Each disappointment, when viewed through the lens of growth, becomes a stepping stone toward a better version of yourself. So, the next time you encounter a reality check, let it empower you. With every lesson you learn and every adjustment you make, you're moving closer to the success you're capable of achieving. Life's greatest victories often come not despite the challenges but because of them. Keep moving forward—you've got this.

Remember, disappointment is temporary, but the lessons it teaches you can last a lifetime. In fact, sometimes it's the detours that lead us to better destinations than we could have imagined. When one door closes, it's often because another, better one is waiting for you to walk through it. So, don't be discouraged when things don't go according to plan. Instead, trust that this detour is just a stepping stone on the path to something even better.

And here's the kicker: disappointment doesn't define you. It's what you do after the disappointment that shapes who you become. Will you let it keep you down, or will you use it to fuel your next move? The choice is yours. So, next time you face disappointment, remember—it's not the end. It's simply a detour on the road to something greater. Embrace it, learn from it, and keep moving forward. Because, in the end, disappointment is just a detour—not a dead end. And the journey ahead is full of endless possibilities waiting for you.

It's easy to fall into a spiral of disappointment, thinking that things couldn't possibly get worse. When things don't turn out the way we hoped, our minds often race with the worst-case scenarios—imagining every possible negative outcome, convincing ourselves that we're at rock bottom. But here's a shift in perspective: What if things could have been much worse, but they didn't? What if the disappointment you're facing is actually life saving you from a greater, more devastating outcome?

In moments of disappointment, it's tempting to dwell on the idea of how much worse things could have been. But what if we flipped the script and recognized that disappointment might actually be a form of protection—a gentle nudge steering us away from a path that could have led to something far more challenging or even harmful? Often, we focus so intently on what we didn't achieve or what didn't work out that we fail to see the potential difficulties we might have avoided. Disappointment, in its essence, can be a signal that something wasn't meant for us or that a better opportunity lies ahead. It saves us from investing time, energy, or emotion into situations that might have drained us further. When viewed this way, disappointment transforms from a source of frustration to a hidden safeguard, guiding us toward a better fit, a brighter opportunity, or a more fulfilling journey. Instead of resisting it, embracing disappointment allows us to see its protective power and trust the process of life unfolding in our favor.

The key is to recognize that disappointment, though painful, is not always a reflection of failure. It's a form of protection. While you may not always see the bigger picture in the moment, in time, the dots begin to connect. Disappointment is a way of ensuring that you are not bound to a situation that could cause you more harm, stress, or unhappiness down the line.

It's a humbling thought: What if the situation you're in, no matter how difficult it seems, is a way of life sparing you from something far worse?

So, the next time disappointment knocks on your door, pause for a moment to ask yourself: Could this be a blessing in disguise? What if things didn't go the way I hoped because something better is waiting for me? What if this setback is the universe's way of sparing me from something worse?

Life, with all its twists and turns, often works in mysterious ways. The disappointments we face today may seem like failures, but they are often the unseen forces working in our favor, guiding us toward a path that is better suited to our growth and happiness.

In the end, it's important to remember that not every disappointment is a setback. Sometimes, it's a lesson in patience, a reminder to trust the process, and a sign that things could have been much worse but weren't. Embrace that reality, and let it give you the strength to move forward with faith that better things lie ahead.

CHAPTER XIX

# Why to Worry When the Unknown is Full of Possibilities

The unknown is not a void—it's a field of untapped potential. Think of it as the horizon at sunrise, full of colors yet to unfold. You may not see what lies beyond, but you know it's there, waiting to reveal itself. The unknown is not an enemy; it's a partner in your growth, offering you a world of opportunities disguised as uncertainty.

When you were a child, the unknown wasn't scary—it was exciting. Every first, from riding a bike to making a new friend, started with a step into the unfamiliar. Back then, your curiosity outshined your fear, and the idea of "what's next?" was enough to push you forward. But somewhere along the way, as responsibilities piled up and expectations grew, the unknown started feeling like a risk rather than an adventure.

The unknown is a gift. It's the place where you create, discover, and redefine yourself. Unlike the well-trodden paths, it's yours to shape. The uncertainty that comes with it is just a small price to pay for the infinite possibilities it holds.

Picture an artist standing before a blank canvas, their palette filled with vibrant colors. There's no sketch to follow, no predefined outcome—just an expanse of white waiting to come alive. For some, this blankness might feel paralyzing, a space filled with questions like, "What if I mess up?" or "What if it doesn't turn out right?" But for the artist, it's a world of possibility. The empty canvas isn't intimidating; it's an invitation.

Every brushstroke, bold or hesitant, becomes part of the story they're creating. The colors might blend unexpectedly, and lines may wander off course, but that's where the beauty lies—in the unpredictability. It's not about perfection but about embracing the journey of creation.

In much the same way, life hands you a series of blank canvases. Each choice, every step into the unknown, is your brushstroke. Some decisions might seem messy at first, and others might surprise you with their brilliance. Even missteps can add a layer of depth, giving your story a richness it wouldn't otherwise have. The unknown isn't something to fear; it's a medium through which you craft your unique masterpiece.

Instead of asking, "What if I fail?" ask yourself, "What could I create?" Shift your perspective and see the unknown for what it truly is: a chance to paint a life that's authentically yours.

Seeing Through a New Lens. We often treat the unknown like a dark tunnel, focusing solely on the uncertainty at the other end. But what if we saw it differently? What if the unknown wasn't a void to fear but a kaleidoscope—a constantly shifting array of patterns, colors, and perspectives? It's unpredictable, yes, but also bursting with potential and beauty.

Consider the night sky. At first glance, it might appear as a random scattering of stars—distant, incomprehensible, and overwhelming in its vastness. Yet, when you look closer and start to connect the dots, constellations emerge, each with its own story and significance. The stars haven't changed; your perspective has. What once seemed like chaos reveals itself as a stunning tapestry, reminding us that beauty and meaning often lie in what we don't initially understand.

The unknown in life works the same way. Each unfamiliar step, like a star in the sky, might seem isolated and insignificant. But as you move forward and take the time to connect the experiences, they form a bigger picture—one you couldn't see from the starting line. It's in embracing this unpredictability that you uncover the magic hidden within.

Imagine navigating a new phase of life—a career change, a relationship, or a personal challenge. The road ahead might feel scattered and unclear, much like staring into the vast cosmos. But as you journey onward, each decision and experience lights up another star in your personal constellation, creating a map that's uniquely yours. The unknown isn't there to confuse you; it's there to guide you toward growth, adventure, and self-discovery.

By shifting our perspective and choosing to see the unknown as a kaleidoscope or a starry sky, we empower ourselves to find patterns, purpose, and even joy in what we can't yet predict. Instead of fearing what's ahead, we can marvel at its potential, knowing that every step we take brings us closer to uncovering something extraordinary.

Curiosity is your greatest ally when stepping into the unknown. It shifts the narrative from "What if it goes wrong?" to "What might I learn?" Think of scientists who dedicate their lives to asking questions without knowing the answers. Their curiosity leads them to breakthroughs not because they avoided the unknown, but because they embraced it.

Apply this mindset to your own life. Instead of fearing a career change, ask yourself, "What skills might I develop?" Instead of worrying about starting a new hobby, wonder, "What joy could this bring me?" Curiosity doesn't erase the uncertainty, but it reframes it into something exciting rather than terrifying.

Facing the unknown doesn't have to feel overwhelming. Here's a simple exercise to make it more manageable. Start by closing your eyes and visualizing all the positive outcomes that could arise from stepping into uncertainty. Instead of fixating on what could go wrong, focus on what could go right. Next, reframe your fear by shifting your mindset. Rather than asking, "What if I fail?" consider, "What's the best lesson I could learn from this experience?" Finally, take a small step forward. You don't have to make a giant leap; even the smallest action can build confidence and start to reveal the path ahead. By breaking down the unknown into these manageable pieces, you'll find it's not as intimidating as it seems.

The 11:11 Wish Perspective.

You know how people stop everything when they see 11:11 on the clock? They close their eyes, make a wish, and believe, even if just for a moment, that something magical might happen. It's quirky, it's hopeful, and, let's be honest, it's a little random. But what if we approached the unknown in life with the same playful optimism?

Instead of dreading the uncertainty of what's next, treat it like your personal "11:11 moment." Sure, the path ahead is uncharted, but that's where the magic lives. When you step into the unknown, it's like making a wish—you're trusting that something good is waiting for you, even if you can't see it yet.

And here's the funny part: at least with the unknown, you don't have to frantically check your phone for the right time to act. Life is constantly throwing 11:11 moments your way—those opportunities to wish, hope, and take a leap of faith. The unknown isn't asking for perfection; it's just asking for a little courage and a dash of imagination.

So the next time you catch yourself overthinking about the uncertainty ahead, pause and make a mental "wish" instead. But don't stop there—take a step, no matter how small, toward making that wish come true. Who knows? The unknown might just grant you something even better than you imagined.

Your Invitation to the Unwritten. Life isn't a pre-written book. It's an open journal, and the unknown is the next blank page. Yes, the uncertainty might feel uncomfortable, but it's also where the most meaningful stories begin.

So, the next time you face the unknown, don't turn away. Walk into it with curiosity and courage. Treat it as a partner in your journey, a collaborator in the story you're writing. The unknown doesn't hold you back; it invites you forward.

When you embrace it, you don't just discover what's out there—you discover who you are. And isn't that the greatest adventure of all?

CHAPTER XX

# Why to Worry When Rejection Leads to Redirection

Rejection. The very word feels like a heavy door slamming shut, leaving you standing on the outside, questioning your worth. Whether it's a missed opportunity, an unreciprocated love, or a denied dream, rejection stings. It chips away at our confidence, leaving us with lingering doubts.

Rejection—it's like that one relative who shows up uninvited to family gatherings. Nobody wants it, and yet, at some point, we all have to deal with it. Whether it's getting turned down for a job, being ghosted by someone you confessed your feelings to, or not making the cut for a position you dreamed of, rejection stings. But let's be honest, do we really let it stop us?

Think about it. Imagine you've been rejected in a job interview. Does that mean you'll never apply for another job again? Of course not! You dust off your resume, add a few more buzzwords, and hit "submit" on the next listing. Or maybe you proposed to someone you adore, and they hit you with, "I think we're better off as friends." Ouch, right? But does that mean you'll swear off love forever and start a lifelong romance with your couch and Netflix? Absolutely not! You'll probably cry, eat a tub of ice cream, and then swipe right on someone else.

And what about being rejected from a post or position you really wanted? Maybe you didn't win the election or weren't chosen for that leadership role. Does that mean you'll stop dreaming big? Nope. You'll find another path, another opportunity, and keep pushing forward.

Here's the funny thing about rejection: It's like bad Wi-Fi. It's annoying and frustrating, but you keep refreshing the page because you know the connection will come back eventually. Rejection might make you want to hide under a blanket and avoid the world, but deep down, you know you'll try again.

The Beauty of "No". A "no" can be liberating. It saves you from settling for less than what you deserve. It forces you to pause, reassess, and recalibrate. It's a chance to build resilience, to strengthen your belief in yourself, and to prepare for what's next.

Imagine a door closing in front of you. It's natural to fixate on that door, mourning its closure. But what if, instead, you turned around to see an open window? That's rejection—it closes one door but often opens another, sometimes in ways you couldn't have anticipated.

The key to handling rejection is resilience, and building it is simpler than you might think. Start by finding humor in the situation—sometimes, laughter really is the best medicine. Humor lightens the emotional load and reminds you not to take life too seriously. Next, look for the lesson hidden in the rejection. Maybe it's a nudge to improve your skills, develop patience, or accept that some things aren't meant for you. Every rejection carries wisdom if you're willing to see it. Finally, remember that rejection isn't the end of your story; it's just a pause before the next chapter. Dust yourself off, gather your courage, and try again. Rejection is not the finale. It's just an intermission before your next act.

Fear of rejection is a universal experience, one that often holds us back from pursuing what we truly want. It's the voice in our head that says, "What if they say no?" or "What if I'm not good enough?" This fear stems from our innate desire for acceptance and belonging, making rejection feel like a personal failure. But the truth is, rejection is rarely about us—it's about circumstances, timing, or someone else's perspective. While the fear of rejection can be paralyzing, it's important to remember that every "no" is a step closer to a "yes." It's not a reflection of our worth but a redirection toward where we're truly meant to be. Embracing the possibility of rejection frees us to take risks, grow, and discover opportunities that fear would otherwise keep hidden.

Rejection, though often difficult to experience, plays a crucial role in building confidence. Each rejection is an opportunity to learn, adapt, and grow stronger. Rather than seeing it as a setback, embracing rejection as a natural part of the journey allows individuals to develop resilience. The more one faces rejection and continues to pursue their goals despite it, the more they understand their own capabilities and improve their approach. Over time, this builds a sense of self-assurance, showing that failure is not an end, but a stepping stone to success. With each experience, confidence grows not from avoiding rejection, but from knowing how to handle it and move forward.

When we find ourselves in the position of having to reject someone, it can feel just as difficult as being rejected. The discomfort of disappointing another person often brings anxiety, especially when we recognize the potential pain our decision may cause. Whether it's a job candidate, a colleague, or a friend, rejecting someone can stir feelings of guilt or doubt. However, rejecting others doesn't mean we are causing harm—it simply means we are setting boundaries, being honest, and ensuring that the situation is aligned with our needs and values.

When we are the ones delivering rejection, the key is to do so with empathy, kindness, and clarity. The goal is not to tear someone down but to guide them toward better opportunities that are more suited to their journey. Think of it like a gardener pruning a plant—while it may seem harsh in the moment, it helps the plant grow stronger and healthier in the long run. Whether you are rejecting a job candidate because they aren't the right fit or turning down a request because it doesn't align with your values, the goal is to be respectful and gentle while ensuring both parties are redirected toward paths that suit them better.

Rejection is not the opposite of success; it's a step toward it. It builds character, deepens empathy, and strengthens resolve. Every successful person you admire has faced rejection. The difference? They didn't stop. They embraced the redirection, trusting that their journey would lead them where they were meant to be.

The next time rejection knocks on your door, welcome it. Say thank you for the lessons it brings. Trust that it's carving a path uniquely yours—a path filled with opportunities you never imagined, relationships you'll cherish, and growth you'll be proud of.

Rejection isn't failure; it's a force that pushes you forward. And in the grand scheme of your life, every "no" is leading you to a more fulfilling "yes."

So, why worry? Rejection isn't the end; it's a beautiful redirection toward where you truly belong.

# Conclusion

As we turn the final page of this book, I hope you've nodded in agreement, laughed a little, and found comfort in the shared human experience woven through each chapter. We've navigated through the labyrinth of worries that life throws at us—whether it's the fear of rejection, the pressure of making the right decisions, the struggle with self-doubt, or the uncertainty of the unknown. Each worry may have once felt like an immovable mountain, but together, we've explored how they're actually stepping stones on the path to a fulfilled life.

From worrying about fitting into the right "league" to battling imposter syndrome, from the fear of failure to the uneasiness of taking the first step into the unknown, we've dissected these challenges and flipped the script. Each chapter is a reminder that life isn't about avoiding worries—it's about learning how to embrace them, grow through them, and keep moving forward.

If there's one message to take from this journey, it's this: your worries don't define you; your actions do. Whether it's rejection steering you toward new opportunities, decisions shaping your destiny, or the unknown unveiling its hidden magic, every moment is part of your unique story. And the beauty of life lies in its imperfections and unpredictability.

I believe we're all fighting for the lives we dream of, and here's the truth: you're going to achieve it. It might not look exactly as you imagined, but trust the journey—it's leading you exactly where you need to go. So, let go of your worries, and hold on to the belief that you are capable, deserving, and resilient.

Keep working, keep dreaming, and keep trusting yourself. The life you want is waiting for you—just a few courageous steps beyond the horizon of your worries.

# About The Author

Hi there! I'm a 21-year-old girl on the verge of graduating as a Computer Engineer—a path I never thought I'd take but somehow found my way through. At one point, I didn't even want to be an engineer, but life, with its unexpected twists, led me here. Along the way, I discovered my love for stories, books, and words.

I've devoured everything from motivational books to fictional tales that transport you to magical worlds. It's this love for reading that planted the seed of passion for writing my own book. And here I am, turning that dream into reality with the book you've just read!

Oh, and yes—I am cute, and I adore cats (seriously, how could you not?). In fact, let's talk about the bonus "Cat Rule" I've created for you as a token of appreciation for being here after completing the book.

The Bonus CAT Rule: Life Lessons from Our Feline Friends

**C – Confidence**

Cats exude confidence. They strut around like they own the place, jump from ridiculous heights without hesitation, and always land on their feet. Their self-assurance is a lesson for us all: trust yourself, take risks, and face challenges knowing you'll find a way to land gracefully.

**A – Adaptability**

Cats are masters of adapting to their surroundings, whether it's a new home or finding a sunny spot to nap. Life throws curveballs, and adaptability is key to thriving. Be like a cat—embrace change, learn from setbacks, and keep moving forward.

**T – Tenacity**

Ever seen a cat trying to open a door or catch a laser pointer? They never give up. Their tenacity is admirable and a reminder to stay persistent, even when things seem tough. Success comes to those who keep pushing, just like a cat finally catching its "prey."

**S – Self-Reliance**

Cats are fiercely independent. They trust their instincts and figure things out on their own. While it's okay to lean on others for support, being self-reliant gives you the power to take charge of your life and decisions.

Channel your inner feline: walk with confidence, embrace change, be tenacious, and trust yourself. And don't forget to curl up in a cozy spot and rest when life feels overwhelming.

To my fellow cat lovers and dreamers, I hope this book brought a smile to your face, a spark to your thoughts, and a little courage to your heart. You've got this!

# Sneak Peek Into The Next Chapter: Snip, Snip, And A Love Story

It all started with a pair of scissors. Yep, you read that right. On New Year's Day, I chopped off my long, beloved hair—the hair I'd spent years loving, flaunting, and treating like royalty. Everyone gasped, "Why did you cut your hair? You loved it so much!" And honestly? The instant regret hit hard. Like, did I just cut off my identity?!

But here's the twist: this wasn't just about a haircut. It was my bold (and slightly impulsive) declaration to embrace change, challenge myself, and step into the new year as a stronger, braver, and slightly shorter-haired version of myself. Funny? Definitely. Dramatic? Absolutely. Symbolic? Oh, you bet!

Now, here's where things get exciting. That little haircut meltdown inspired something big. Picture this: a fictional love story featuring a character who's quirky, imperfect, and absolutely unforgettable—kind of like me with a fresh lob haircut. Did I cut my hair to channel my inner writer and finish this book? Maybe. Did it work? You'll have to read it to find out.

So, while I'm busy styling this new look (and occasionally crying over it), I'm also crafting a love story that will steal your heart. Stay tuned—you won't want to miss this one.

Stay Connected!

I'd love to hear your thoughts on this book and connect with fellow dreamers and readers.

Follow me on Instagram: @bookwormshruti for more bookish content, inspiration, and updates on my writing journey!

Happy reading and keep chasing your dreams!

• • •

www.ingramcontent.com/pod-product-compliance
Lightning Source LLC
LaVergne TN
LVHW041105150826
845673LV00007B/1930

* 9 7 9 8 8 9 6 9 9 8 0 4 4 *